Journey to Freedom is convicting, p[...] Chad does a tremendous job in sho[...] the body of Christ should look like.

Luke Milam
Director, Time on the Mountain
Ministries

Journey to Freedom, by Chad Barrett, challenges men to be men of integrity and men of authenticity. The temptations men face are powerful, and the battles men fight are difficult. Chad does not settle for surface answers to deep struggles. He calls for an end to faking spirituality and hiding sin. *Journey to Freedom* shows how authentic spiritual fellowship with a few transparent men can help in resisting and overcoming temptation. He also shares guidelines for recovering from moral failure. *Journey to Freedom* is a call to men to cultivate and champion authentic fellowship that can help prevent moral failures. I believe Chad Barrett's book can make a significant impact in the lives of men who act on it and in the lives of men they care about.

Dr. Harlan D. Betz,
Pastor of Grace Chapel Castle Rock
Author of *Setting the Stage for Eternity*

Nothing is more enjoyable than reading a book by an author who practices what he preaches. That is why Chad's book is one every man would be helped by reading. Chad pleads for authenticity among men—the kind of authenticity that merits reward when we see the Savior face to face. He knows what that kind of authenticity demands and calls upon the church to help men grow in their fellowship with God and others. But Chad is one of those authentic people himself—a "what-you-see-is-what-you-get" type of person. I know. I have watched him as a friend and been privileged to have him as a student. His passionate plea and "how to" advice will start you on a road to freedom—a freedom that only comes when we let God and others help us be the men God wants us to be.

Dr. Larry Moyer
President/CEO, EvanTell Inc.

Chad Barrett talks straight. An unapologetic veteran of every man's battle, Chad has written a life-guide every Christian guy should read. *Journey to Freedom* is like a tank of pure oxygen delivered to men who've been buried alive.

Nate Larkin
Founder of the Samson Society
Author of *Samson and the Pirate Monks: Calling Men to Authentic Brotherhood*

Journey to Freedom

The Pursuit of Authentic Fellowship among Men

J. Chad Barrett, Sr.

WestBow
PRESS
A DIVISION OF THOMAS NELSON

WestBow Press books may be ordered through booksellers or by contacting:

WestBow Press
A Division of Thomas Nelson
1663 Liberty Drive
Bloomington, IN 47403
www.westbowpress.com
1-(866) 928-1240

Because of the dynamic nature of the Internet, any web addresses or links contained in this book may have changed since publication and may no longer be valid. The views expressed in this work are solely those of the author and do not necessarily reflect the views of the publisher, and the publisher hereby disclaims any responsibility for them.

Any people depicted in stock imagery provided by Thinkstock are models, and such images are being used for illustrative purposes only.

Certain stock imagery © Thinkstock.

ISBN: 978-1-4497-1633-2 (sc)
ISBN: 978-1-4497-1635-6 (dj)
ISBN: 978-1-4497-1634-9 (e)

Library of Congress Control Number: 2011927540

Printed in the United States of America

WestBow Press rev. date: 4/27/2011

To Jonathan,
May You Live Above the Common

CONTENTS

PREFACE   IX
ACKNOWLEDGEMENTS   XI
INTRODUCTION   XIII

SECTION 1:   THE CALL TO JOURNEY   1

1. THE FREEDOM IN BECOMING HIS METOCHOI   3
2. THE FREEDOM TO HAVE AUTHENTIC FELLOWSHIP   8
3. FREEDOM COMES FROM SHARING CHRIST'S PASSION   23
4. FREEDOM COMES FROM TWO INGREDIENTS   35

SECTION 2:   STARTING THE JOURNEY   49

5. DRAWING UP BATTLE PLANS   51
6. THE SHADOW AND THE CHAMPION   70
7. CHAMPIONS *PREP*ARE FOR BATTLE   79
8. THERE'S FREEDOM ON THE OTHER SIDE   104
9. DON'T FORGET THE OTHERS   132

DISCUSSION QUESTIONS   139
ENDNOTES   143

PREFACE

Christian men are falling.

Many men in our local churches are currently on the fast track toward destruction. Many are trapped in self-made cages, hiding themselves in darkness, hoping no one sees where they really are, and at the same time earnestly desiring for someone to set them free. You might very well be one of these men. The interesting thing is that I haven't even mentioned what it is that's causing men to fall. But, nonetheless, the words I have just typed on this paper are calling your name, aren't they?

You know exactly the feeling of being snagged by temptation, overcome by its powerful pull, and trapped by sin's cords. Ironically, those cords that have you trapped are the same cords that look so appealing at the same time. Your flesh longs for them, yet all the while they are pulling you down deeper and deeper into the pit of destruction. You wonder when your time will come. When will you hit the bottom, and what will you lose when you get there? Isn't it time something is done? The Church must take drastic measures. But what can and should we do?

Over the years, I have grown deeply passionate about seeing Christian men enter into the joyous wonder of authentic fellowship with God and with one another. I have grown passionate about seeing men in our churches experience the freedom from the power of sin to which this authenticity in fellowship can lead. I'm concerned for

Christian fathers and their influence on their sons and daughters. I'm concerned for Christian husbands and their leadership roles in their homes. And my heart is broken over pastors and laymen who are falling morally and losing their ministries and families.

I'm convinced the impact of Christian men, in general, is dwindling in our effectiveness as real leaders in our homes and churches. I'm convinced this is because of a combination of two things: 1) a lack of biblical influence within many of our churches for men to become what we are supposed to become, and 2) a tremendous increase of the worldly influence produced by internet pornography sites, by the struggle of the love of money, and by the temptation to neglect our families. These latter three things are the major areas in which, according to Steve Farrar in his book *Finishing Strong*, Christian men tend to be "ambushed": the ambush of another woman, the ambush of money, and the ambush of a neglected family. These are the three most common things that bind men. It is time that we men do something that will help one another break these bonds. It is time we men begin our journey to freedom together.

This book comes from a heart heavily burdened by several friends who have fallen into sexual sins and are presently suffering the consequences of them. It comes from a passionate desire to help churches change the way their people, especially their men, view one another: no longer as casual acquaintances but as true friendships. It comes from a healthy fear that I could become just like one of my fallen friends.

What you will read here shows the biblical mandate of authentic fellowship in our local churches and teaches how to develop this authenticity among men. These are proven ideas and methods. I, and many others, have put them into practice, and they work. My prayer is that this book becomes a tool to inspire, motivate, and challenge men in local churches to work effectively toward developing authentic fellowship that is sure to further them along in their journey to freedom. I am convinced that the journey to freedom is paved with God's Word and lined with God's people.

ACKNOWLEDGEMENTS

First, and foremost, my Savior has saved me from the penalty of sin, He continues to save me from the power of sin, and one day He will save me from the presence of sin. To You, my Jesus, I am eternally grateful!

My wonderful wife, Melissa, has more than fulfilled my dream of a wife. Thank you for loving me the way you do. I have married out of my league—you complete me! You're my 1, and I love you.

My Mom and Dad have (and continue to) instilled in me the mind of Christ. You are still teaching me how to be a godly husband and father. Being your son has been a great honor. I love you, both.

Having dedicated this book to my son, Jonathan, I acknowledge that my four children (including Kristina, Caroline, and Katherine) have enhanced my life more than I can express in words. You are a priceless treasure—a crown for me to wear proudly. I am committed to lead you to freedom.

My editor and friend, Jennifer Bonvillain, has put forth hours upon hours of dedicated work for this project. Without complaint, she has made this book a top priority, along with being a great wife to Greg and a great mother to her children. Thanks Jennifer! You're the best!

To my 70, 12, and 3: Thank you for your patience with me, your support of me, and your encouragement to me.

To Greg Oliver. Your continuing journey to freedom inspires me. Your friendship is cherished. And your fellowship is more than appreciated. Thank you for your contribution to this project!

To you, the reader: Many others have written greater works on this topic. I am grateful that you have decided to give this book a try. It is my earnest prayer that it will spark in you a passion for purity and integrity which will be contagious in your church. Thank you.

INTRODUCTION

Jack's Story

Jack is a Christian. He trusted Christ as his Savior when he was 7 years old at Vacation Bible School. Growing up wasn't that bad. He and his younger brother fought a little. His mom and dad worked a lot, but Jack enjoyed the things he had: his video games, his motorcycle, and his friends.

His family took great vacations each year. One summer, when Jack was 13, they went to Hawaii. It was about that time that Jack really began to notice the beauty of the female body. On the beaches of Hawaii, Jack noticed some very nice-looking ladies wearing string bikinis. He realized that his dad noticed, too, but Jack never said anything about it. Neither did his dad. Jack's mom pretended to be oblivious to her husband's wandering eyes.

About a month later, Jack spent the night at a friend's house. They were talking about a girl at school who, rumor had it, had been fooling around with several of the boys. Later that evening, Jack's friend told him about an old barn down the road that supposedly had some *Playboy* magazines stashed in the loft. They decided to go check it out.

Having waited until almost midnight, the two boys sneaked out of the house and walked down the road to the old barn. There was no lock on the door, so they entered, climbed up the loft, and began to fish around for anything resembling stacks of paper. After a few minutes, the boys found the magazines wrapped in an old blanket under some hay. They took one and, with a flashlight in hand, thumbed through the pages.

Jack had never seen anything like that before, and it made his heart beat fast and hard. He knew it was wrong to look at these pictures, but there was a strong inner pull to keep turning the pages. After about fifteen minutes, they each took one magazine and ran back to the house.

The next day, Jack hid his new secret treasure in his bag and brought it home. He ran upstairs to his room and stuffed it under his mattress. *Surely no one will find it here,* he thought.

A week later, his mom found it while making his bed and approached his dad with it. His dad said he would take care of Jack, but he never did. Instead, his dad hid the magazine in his office at work along with the rest of his own stash of pornographic material. Jack's dad never confronted him about the magazine. In fact, Jack's dad never talked with him about anything related to sex, lust, or masturbation. Jack learned everything he knew from his friends at school.

Jack is now 32 years old. He's married with two kids—a 5-year-old son and a 3-year-old daughter. He is an engineer for a successful oil company, and his wife is a nurse at a nearby hospital. They live in a beautiful home in an upscale neighborhood, and they attend a medium-sized church in their town each Sunday where his wife teaches the 3- and 4-year-old children's Sunday school class and Jack helps out with the youth group.

Jack has been viewing porn on the internet since his college days. It has become a habit he can't seem to break. The habit is beginning to move him in directions he never thought he would go. There is a 24-hour video store on the way home from work. He feels the tug of temptation each time he drives home from the office.

He and his wife are part of a small group that meets on Wednesday nights. The leader is a seminary student, and he facilitates some great Bible studies. Jack learns about the attributes of God. He learns about the importance and power of prayer. He learns how to be wise with his finances. And he learns some great Bible study methods.

He and his wife really enjoy the small group sessions. They are close friends with another couple who also has two kids.

Jack attends some of the men's ministry's events in his church, but usually only the ones that include basketball, fishing, hunting, or when they go to pro baseball games. Sometimes he attends a men's fellowship dinner at church.

The guys in the men's ministry are nice guys. They all work hard, love their wives, raise great kids, and always seem to have it all together. But Jack doesn't have it all together. He tries to put up a front, like all the other guys have, that portrays him as a godly, Christlike man. And in some ways, he really tries to be godly. But he continues his downward spiral toward utter destruction, losing control of his thoughts and actions. He never hears any talk of other guys in his church struggling with this sin, so he must handle it alone.

He thought about telling his pastor or some other respectable man at church, until last year when the music pastor was caught in an adulterous affair. The leadership told the music pastor not to return to the church—at least this is what Jack heard through the grapevine. No one has seen the music pastor since, and nothing more has ever been said about the issue.

Little does Jack know that this time next year his wife and kids will be away for a week to visit her parents in another state. Jack will stay behind due to work. While they are away, he will visit that 24-hour video store. He will be torn up inside, but the next day he will visit again.

Two years from now, he will have his first encounter with a prostitute. This lifestyle will continue for the next three years, until one of his fellow church members will see his car pull over to pick up a young lady who is not his wife. The church member will quickly bring the news to the pastor.

Jack's pastor will tell him that he's not really a Christian, because *genuine* faith would prevent him from this kind of sin. His wife will leave him and take the kids with her. Jack will stop attending church, and no one will call him because Jack is a sinner. Most of the people at church will start avoiding him anyway, and Jack will get tired of the rumors and gossip spreading about him and his family. Some of the gossip will be that Jack's problem was his wife's fault.

Jack will spend the next few years taking addictive medication just to cope with the pain he has brought upon himself. By the time Jack is in his mid-forties, he will have been married and divorced again, hooked on drugs, and closing down the strip joints.

Jack will die of alcohol poisoning at age 48. The coroner's office will label Jack's death a suicide.

Jack's son is now 21 years old. His name is David.

He just buried his dad.

And he's addicted to internet porn.

Men, We Really Do Need Help

Not every story ends like that, but many do. This story is actually a conglomerate of several true stories.

As I am writing this, I am sitting in a restaurant waiting for a good friend to go on his break so we can visit. He was once on the pastoral staff in a church and had a marvelous ministry. He has a beautiful wife and three wonderful children. Now, he works the drive-through window of this fast-food restaurant. There's nothing wrong with working at a fast-food restaurant, but it's not meeting his family's financial needs. He lost his position at his church when he fell into temptation.

As Steve Farrar puts it, my friend's sin has taken him farther than he wanted to go, it has kept him longer than he wanted to stay, and it has cost him more than he wanted to pay. My heart deeply feels two things: I am incredibly broken over his crisis, and I am truly frightened because it could very well be me. I admit I've fantasized about doing some of what my friend did, as all men do. I love my friend very much and am so moved to walk by his side through the tough times he has ahead.

The sadder thing is that he is just *one* who got caught. He has repented, is involved in counseling, and is growing more in his relationships with Jesus, his wife, and their children. However, there are many Christian men who have not been caught...yet. They are sinking deeper and deeper in the misery their sin brings. They long for freedom, and they know where to find it.

You might be one of these men. You know that to remove your deceptive façade and let someone see you as you really are could cost you more than you were prepared to pay when you first entered this journey toward destruction. You are torn with a decision—tell all and suffer, or continue in sin and suffer. You know that telling all really would remove a heavy load and continuing in sin would ultimately lead to more destruction. But at least the sin is somewhat fun, and so you deceive yourself again into thinking that you can handle it on your own.

Many men who have fallen have told me they wanted to get caught. They just couldn't hold up anymore underneath the heavy load of sin and deception. Our Christian men—dads, husbands, elders, deacons, Sunday school teachers, pastors, worship leaders, youth pastors, ushers, old men, young men—are bombarded with the temptation to dive into the sin that pursues us all. And many Christian men have endured the train wrecks their sin always, always brings. Why not admit it—we need help.

So the Church of Jesus Christ has the opportunity to help. Therefore we create programs for men. I have to be honest: The men's ministries in which I've been involved usually consist of coffee, donuts, a special speaker giving a short Bible study, sharing prayer requests regarding other people's problems, and a short time of prayer led by a few of the men. While the coffee is good, some friendships are made, and the Bible study is decent, something is lacking. Month after month this program continues its course of maintaining the status quo. Then we become shocked—horrified even—when we hear of a brother in our church who falls. What happened? What could have prevented this?

We may know each other, but let's be honest: We really don't *know* each other, do we? Think about any man in your church. You might know his name. You might know his wife's name. You may even know the number of children he has. But what about his personality and characteristics? What are his pet peeves? What does he struggle with the most? Does he feel alone in his struggles? Is he pursuing the "other woman"? How's his marriage? How's his thought life? Is he indulging in pornography? Is he neglecting his family because of the pursuit of money or position? Is he experiencing intimacy with the Father? Is someone there to help him when he fails? Is there someone to praise him when he overcomes? Are there other men actively showing him how to live a godly life?

Are the men in your church actively entering each others' world? Are the Christian men in your church truly sharpening each other with the Word of God, or is it just another social club that meets once or twice a month? Many churches don't discuss these issues. Guys don't talk about these things, but it's high time we begin.

Don't get me wrong—I love the Church. I love my church! I would be so far down sin's road without it. God established the Church. But is the Church what it should be? Did God create His Church to be what it is today? My heart is heavy with a burden to see our churches break out of their mold of mediocrity to become what they could be and should be.

You see, in church we wear masks. Our masks portray who we want others to see when they greet us on Sunday mornings. Our masks speak of victory over sin, peace in our homes, and peace in our hearts. They proclaim that we have it all together.

In church there are members who don't lust, don't view porn on the internet or television, don't abuse spouses, don't flirt with other women at work, and don't fudge on their taxes. In church there are no liars, no thieves, no idolaters, no adulterers, and no drunkards. The only apparent problems members of our churches face are physical illnesses because that is usually all that is mentioned.

It's so sad—deep inside we know we all struggle with various sins, but we aren't allowed to talk about it. Both men and women are guilty of this. Youth groups are guilty of this. We get together for our Bible studies to learn about God, but we don't get inside the world of one another so we can see God. In church we don't let anyone inside our real lives. We don't bring up the obvious and deal with it together. We deceive ourselves into thinking that we have to deal with our struggles alone. But every time we try, we fail. There is no place for us to bring up the obvious. There is no place for us to open the door of our true selves for others to see what we are really like on the inside. There is no place for real healing. Is there?

If Jesus is the Head of the Church (and He is!) and His Word tells us to bear with one another, carry one another's burdens, and love one another the way Christ loves us, but we don't know one another well enough to do these things, then the Body is not following its Head. How can we carry one another's burdens when there isn't a place for one to share what his burdens are?

The fact is, we don't talk about our burdens. We keep our burdens hidden in the dark, hoping and praying that they will just go away. But when a man's burden—especially when it involves a sin—raises its ugly head, he's all alone to defend himself. He falls because there is no one by his side to offer support, guidance, and direction. God created the Church to spread His gospel, but we aren't standing on the gospel because we are too busy stumbling over our own burdens. Guys don't talk about these things, but it's high time we do. This doesn't come easily for us. What does this look like? How do we establish this kind of authentic ministry in our churches?

This book is meant to tackle this problem of isolation among Christian men in our churches. The things that are mentioned in this introduction will be expounded upon throughout this book. It is my prayer that you find this to be a tool to use to establish a men's ministry in your church that is authentic or to make the necessary changes in a ministry that already exists. Either way, it's time for Christian men to be free—free from the power of sin. Let's begin our journey to freedom together!

SECTION ONE:

THE CALL TO JOURNEY

CHAPTER ONE

THE FREEDOM IN BECOMING HIS METOCHOI

What Is a Metochoi?

I took two years of Greek at Southeastern Bible College in Birmingham, AL. Unfortunately, I'm quite rusty. Yet over the years I have used what I learned, and one word that has stuck in my mind for so long is the word to which this entire chapter is dedicated. That Greek word is *metochoi* (me-tuh-koy), and with it is carried the wonderful idea of freedom.

But freedom here, like anywhere else it is found, does not come easily, nor is it cheap. Becoming a metochoi requires much effort. Men who are metochoi are real men, weak men, strong men, honest men, loyal men, and faithful men. Becoming a metochoi can't be done alone because the word includes the idea of *togetherness*. Men who are metochoi don't give up—they persevere *together*. They don't lose very often, because they fight *together*. They overcome, and overcomers overcome together—never alone.

"So what is a *metochoi?*" you ask. Well, it's a wonderful word! It's a motivation and a joyous pursuit. It's a challenge and a daily goal. It's not a thing to do; it's a state of being. And it's found in the book of Hebrews. Chapter 3:12-14 to be exact.

> ^{12}**Beware, brethren, lest there be in any of you an evil heart of unbelief in departing from the living God; ^{13}but exhort one another daily, while it is called *"Today,"* lest any of you be hardened through the deceitfulness of sin. ^{14}For we have become partakers of Christ if we hold the beginning of our confidence steadfast to the end.**

Let's do a little background here. The recipients of the book of Hebrews were Jewish Christians who were second-guessing their conversion to Christianity. (We know they were Christians because the author called them "brethren.") They were being persuaded by the Judaizers (Jews who still held to the Mosaic Law) to return to and abide under the Mosaic Law. They were being bombarded by this temptation and therefore needed encouragement to continue in the faith. The author told them of the importance of *togetherness*, and he stated the motivation for enduring—to become a partaker of Christ!

Can you imagine being a new Jewish Christian during those days? You've been raised to believe a certain way all your life, and now things are so different. You placed your trust in Jesus as the Messiah, the Chosen One Who paid for your sins by dying on the cross and rising from the dead. Yet now so many of your friends are challenging your new relationship with Christ. Perhaps even your family members disown you, unless you recant. Life had to be hard for a new Jewish Christian. Thus, the book of Hebrews was written.

Being a partaker of Christ is not automatic for every believer. It's conditional. The author states that "we," including himself in the process, "become partakers of Christ *if* we hold the beginning of our confidence steadfast to the end." The "if" is conditional upon the believers (the Jewish Christians as well as the author) keeping their confidence in God. The Jewish believers were losing confidence that Jesus was, indeed, the Messiah due to the persuasion of unbelieving Jews. He provided his letter of exhortation and warning to persuade these believers to exhort one another to become "partakers of Christ."

The word the author used for "partakers" was *metochoi*. It's a common Greek word that also means "companion." In business terms it could be translated "associate." Even King David had these—they were his "mighty men." So the author of Hebrews was exhorting those believers not to fall into sin, but to continue in the faith. They would become close associates, close companions with Jesus—experiencing intimate fellowship with the Messiah.

Metochoi is the word for a believer who enters into the intimate fellowship with Christ that He desires of us all. And it's not easy. To partake with Christ is to enter into His suffering. Christ suffered while on the earth. He suffered ridicule, slander, and disloyalty. He suffered temptation. He suffered spiritually, emotionally, mentally, and physically. Ministering authentically to people opens the door for these things. But He continued. He persevered. He endured. And He calls us to partake with Him. When we do, we are His close companions!

And it's not just His suffering that we partake of when we become partakers of Christ; it's also His joy, His peace, His work, His goodness, His mind, His heart, His will, His passion! It's His freedom that we share. That's deep fellowship with Jesus. And it takes effort on our part.

It's a "Together" Word

Did you notice what the author said about exhorting one another daily? Becoming His metochoi requires *togetherness*. It requires the exhortation from one another each day. In fact, without the exhortation from one another daily, it is likely that we will become hardened through the deceitfulness of sin.

Personally, I'm a master at deceiving myself. Think about the first part of this passage again: "Beware, brethren, lest there be in any of you an evil heart of unbelief in departing from the living God."

I have a few friends who would say that this is referring to unbelievers because *real* Christians do not have "unbelief," and they don't depart from the living God. Yet those same friends of mine sing in church the song that says, "Prone to wander, Lord I feel it; prone to leave the God I love" (*Come Thou Fount*).

To be honest with you, I am prone to have a heart that becomes evil. It's evil when I lust. I am prone to have a heart of unbelief. I don't trust in God's promises. I am prone to leave the God I love. Instead, I follow my flesh, which I hate. What I need, as a Christian, is daily exhortation from other Christians who recognize their proneness and potential to distrust but who are, *together* with me, pursuing to become partakers of Christ.

When my heart becomes evil, they don't leave me. When I am walking away from God, they stand in front of me. Why? Because they love me. Because they would want the same from me. Because they are commanded to do this. Because becoming His metochoi can't be done alone. (I am proof of this!) Because we are *together* daily. Metochoi is an *interactive* word—a *together* word. Without the interaction, the authentic fellowship among brethren, we will not become His metochoi.

Not all Christians are Christ's metochoi. Not all believers pursue that intimate fellowship with Jesus and with one another. Many continue in their sin and don't confess. Many wallow in their guilt and shame. Many are passive. Many don't love one another. Many are bitter toward and critical of others. (If you don't believe me, take a good look at your church. In fact, take a good look at yourself.) And many Christian men are trapped in the sin that tempts us all… lust. I've been one of them, and so have you. One of the main reasons this happens is because we are not *together*. We are alone.

It seems like the book of Hebrews is a letter of accountability. These Jewish Christians needed accountability to keep going, to endure, to persevere despite what life brought their way. Don't we all? Intimate fellowship with God is peace, strength, satisfaction, joy, and wonder. It leads to wisdom, maturity, and rewards at the Bema Seat of Christ. It's an abundant life now and a rewarding life in the eternal. It's freedom from guilt and shame, freedom from the consequences of sin, freedom in your marriage, freedom in your parenting, freedom in your minds and hearts. It brings deliverance to you and glory to God.

But it can't be accomplished alone. It isn't meant to be. That's why in Hebrews it also exhorts the readers to "not forsake the gathering of the assembly" (10:25). I'm convinced that true fellowship with God involves true fellowship with one another.

And, quite frankly, guys, we stink at this.

I was recently sent this little story by a friend, and I think it sums it up quite well. I don't know who wrote it, but whoever did wrote something genius.

Every time I am asked to pray, I think of the old deacon who always prayed, "Lord, prop us up on our leanin' side." After hearing him pray that prayer many times, someone asked him why he prayed that prayer so fervently. He answered, "Well sir, you see, it's like this....I got an old barn out back. It's been there a long time, it's withstood a lot of weather, it's gone through a lot of storms, and it's stood for many years. It's still standing, but one day I noticed it was leaning to one side a bit. So I went and got some pine poles and propped it up on its leaning side so it wouldn't fall. Then I got to thinking 'bout that and how much I was like that old barn. I been around a long time, I've withstood a lot of life's storms, I've withstood a lot of bad weather in life, I've withstood a lot of hard times, and I'm still standing, too. But I find myself leaning to one side from time to time, so I like to ask the Lord to prop us up on our leaning side, 'cause I figure a lot of us get to leaning, at times."

Sometimes we get to leaning toward anger, leaning toward bitterness, leaning toward hatred, leaning toward cussing, leaning toward a lot of things that we shouldn't, so we need to pray, "Lord, prop us up on our leaning side," so we will stand straight and tall again, to glorify the Lord. – Author unknown.

We all lean sometimes. When we pray for the good Lord to prop us up, He just might use a pine pole. The truth of the matter is, you very well could be the pine pole that God will use to prop someone else up so he can endure to the end. God uses His people, His Church, to prop one another up. It's called authentic fellowship. It's what the Church needs today. Without it, we perish.

CHAPTER TWO

THE FREEDOM TO HAVE AUTHENTIC FELLOWSHIP

Authentic fellowship is biblical fellowship.

We're talking about freedom here. And the journey to freedom is lined with pine poles. I am thoroughly convinced that part of becoming His metochoi includes entering into the joyous fellowship with other believers. This doesn't happen naturally. It's something learned. I learned it from my parents. Now I realize that not everybody had parents like mine. I don't know why God has blessed me with them, but I'm so glad He did. I'd like to tell you about them.

The Example of My Parents

I grew up in a Christian home. My dad has always been my biggest supporter, best friend, spiritual leader, and qualified authority figure. He has poured his life into me. He entered my world. We have experienced intimate fellowship with each other. It wasn't always perfect, but it was just what I needed to keep me on track. I wasn't always perfect, either. But God used my dad to instill in me the characteristics of a godly man. He didn't just tell me how to live a godly life, he showed me how.

God has blessed me beyond measure through my parents. My mom and dad made home life warm, welcoming, loving, caring, and uplifting. They tell me, even today, that they are my biggest fans, and by their actions, I believe it. When I did well, I was praised. When I screwed up, I was gently and firmly disciplined.

I couldn't lie to my parents…well, usually. The times I did only lasted for a while, and were followed by confession. I believe one reason I had a hard time lying was because my parents built a solid, healthy relationship with me. I hated to hurt them. I knew I could always talk to them about anything. I knew I could always talk to my dad about the things with which guys struggle. I still do today.

Dad taught me many things over the years: perseverance, integrity, compassion, humility. He taught me how to love God, how to love others, how to love my wife, and how to love my children. But one thing that has always stuck deepest within my heart is the one thing that supports those characteristics: Dad taught me how to have authentic fellowship.

As long as I can remember, he has asked me questions. He has always wanted to know my thoughts, my dreams, and my ambitions. I don't remember a time when his *only* question was, "How are you doing?" He has always wanted to know *why*.

In fact, as I was typing this, I received an email from my dad. This week, my son is at Camp Pearl (a church camp in Louisiana where my dad works), and my wife and three daughters are at my wife's parents' home visiting for the week. I told my dad to check up on me while I'm alone at home. These are the times when I'm most tempted to do something stupid. Here is Dad's email to me:

> *Hi Chad,*
> *Just a quick note to check on you to see how you are doing this week. Sure praying for you! Sure love having Jonathan this week…I know you miss your family.*
> *Love you,*
> *Dad*

It doesn't look like much—just a short note. But you know what? I'm doing great this week. This note is huge to me because I knew my dad would be checking in on me. He's called me, too. He really knows me. Dad has always known me because it has been his passion to do so. And my mom has always been as eager to know me as Dad has been. She has been the rock in my life—unwavering and unshakeable.

Now, I don't want you to get the wrong idea. My parents weren't always perfect. They definitely have their flaws, and I could probably fill a few chapters on those! But the thing is, my folks never hid their flaws from us kids. As my brother, sister, and I were growing up, our parents were…well, authentic. They let us know them fully. My dad continues on his quest to know me more even to this day, and—here's the coolest part—the result is intimacy with my heavenly Father.

In fact, I am experiencing intimate fellowship with my heavenly Father today because I have experienced intimate fellowship with my earthly father and mother throughout my life. Dad showed me what biblical fellowship is—what it looks like, what it feels like. Now, as an adult, I am able to sharpen him as he sharpens me. He taught me how to do so. Our relationship is real, it is deep, and it is open. This is fellowship—authentic fellowship. It is the means by which we journey to freedom!

Something Is Missing

I'm not saying that guys who didn't have this kind of mom and dad will not experience fellowship with God. I am saying that everyone needs someone to model and teach them what authentic fellowship is.

Too many men are not free. Too many are suffocating under the heavy load of deception. Too many dads are giving up their families. Too many pastors are giving up their ministries. And too many Christian men are alone in their battles—the battles they face daily, the battles they lose daily. Something is missing.

Growing up with this kind of dad, with these kinds of fellowship experiences, has created a passion within me to be authentic with other Christian men. Second to the family, there is no better place where this genuine fellowship must be experienced than within the

Church. Yet my experience with fellowship in the local church has been far from what I'm convinced God desires it to be.

Growing up in the local church, I found myself asking the questions, "Where's the authenticity here? Why are we not real with each other? Why not voice the obvious about ourselves and deal with it together?" I know many Christian men who were leaders, several of them pastors, in local churches—strong, Bible-believing, solid, doctrinal-teaching churches—who have fallen far enough into the sins that tempt all Christian men so that they have lost their positions as leaders and pastors.

Dads are losing their families. Husbands are losing their wives. Christian men are leaving churches. They are deceiving themselves into escaping that which could and should be leading them to the freedom that Christ died to give us! Something isn't working. Something needs to be fixed.

There's a profound fact that I believe the Church has forgotten, and it has caused severe problems in the spiritual lives of many people—men and women. Simply and plainly put, church is people.

Here are a few questions to ponder. In your church, do your programs exist for your people, or do your people exist for your programs? Is the money in the bank there for people's sake, or do people exist in your church for the money's sake? Is your church a conglomerate of individuals gathering to support the maintenance of the place and its programs, or is your church an active, aggressive, and living organism knowing that it would die without the effective good works of each part of it?

I think something is missing from many churches. It seems as though several local churches have become local empires—local institutions. Some are academic institutions who fail to engage in the lives of one another. Some are social institutions who fail to engage in God's Word. And many just exist. I think that people are missing out on something. I think men in the Church are missing out on something. What we are missing out on is the fact that the bottom line for the Church is people. Plain and simple. The *top goal* for the Church is to glorify God, and this is done when the Church realizes that it's about people.

We are the apple of His eye. Jesus came to deliver people, not to establish Himself in popularity and fame. Jesus died for people, not for a facility. Jesus is coming back for people, not for our extravagant local empires. The Church is people. Ministry is people.

And guess what? Men are people, too. But many men are missing. Some are there, but still missing. Some attend, but are alone. I'm convinced that God has created something very special for His people that is very often misunderstood. I'm convinced this is what Christian men are missing.

I believe this special thing draws men, and it keeps men in the local church. It upholds men, enabling us to stand up tall when life pulls us down. It ties a tight bond around us that is permanent, and its bond is strong and thick. It protects. It never yields. It never fails. Its pillars are *togetherness*, not isolation; *godly love*, not hate; *edification*, not tearing down; *individuality* and *unity*, not legalism nor division.

It is deep, not shallow. Purposeful, not accidental. It's a divinely bestowed phenomenon—mostly hard to accomplish, not easy. But its foundation is the *Savior*, and its finishing touches are *ultimate joy*! Its name is Fellowship, and we must have it. For without it, we will die. The joy, devotion, love, purity, integrity, passion for the gospel, passion for holiness, passion for grace and mercy, passion for God will dry up, and we will die. The sad truth is that many of our churches already have, and they don't even realize it.

But we don't have fellowship because we don't bring up the obvious about ourselves and deal with it together. We don't talk about certain issues. We keep silent.

It's Time to State the Obvious

A few years ago, I was invited to join a school board meeting near Houston, TX. They were seeking pastoral advice for a project they were working on to help encourage kids to stop drinking alcohol.

Before the meeting officially began, most of the board members and pastors/youth pastors had arrived and were getting to know each other. Since we were pastors, the subject of "church" came up. We had all realized that every one of the members of the school board was also a member of one of various churches around the community.

What I found interesting was when the meeting officially began, the talk about church, Jesus, Christianity, God, or anything related to these things was not allowed. Even as pastors, we were encouraged to be "professional" about our beliefs—keep the topic on alcohol and how to prevent kids from abusing it. We were all church members, but we were not allowed to bring up the obvious among ourselves. The meeting was very dry and boring, and everyone knew it. The fun stopped when the meeting began. The fun resumed when we officially closed the meeting.

I find this to resemble church in many ways. Especially as men, there are obvious things among all of us. We all have the same struggles—lust, desire for power, pride, inferiority complexes, and so on—but we don't really talk about these things among the church. Perhaps this is one reason why so many churches are dry and dull. Trust me, go to your church and bring up the subject of sex, and you'll definitely liven things up in your Sunday school class!

When we're at work, we bring up these topics. You don't believe me? I'll prove it. What do the jokes at your workplace usually involve? Should I make the list of struggles again? I'm willing to bet that the men at your place of employment often speak about lusting, their pride in their positions, and their inferiorities (even if it's unintentional). And it's not just because they like to entertain one another with jokes. I'm convinced many of these are underlying confessions to find out whether or not they are alone in their battles. They realize these are battles because these things never produce the results they really want. These things never satisfy. And men end up feeling alone because they are alone—especially in the church. In fact, Christian men may even be more alone in their local churches than they are at their workplaces. We are individuals on the same road called life, but we are driving in our own lanes.

So we come to church, and for some ungodly reason we silence ourselves regarding the things that are usually at the forefront of our lives, the things that are shaping our character, the things that our wives and sons and daughters see consuming our thoughts and actions. But we don't talk about them at church. We don't really talk about them in depth anywhere. We don't talk about pornography addictions, although 70 percent of Christian, church-going men view it repeatedly.[1] We don't talk about "the other woman" at work, even though many Christian guys are entertaining fantasies about them, making plans with them, or even going home late from the office because they've been with them. Men do not talk about their love of money or how they are tempted to cheat on their taxes or steal from work so they can pay their bills during a recession.

We don't bring up the obvious and deal with it together. The truth is that the way to prevent kids from abusing alcohol is to teach them how to be controlled by the Holy Spirit, but I wasn't allowed to bring up that obvious notion.

The truth is that the way to prevent Christian men from falling into sin is to become authentic with one another, but we simply do not bring up the obvious about ourselves and deal with it together. We're too afraid. We're in the dark, and biblical fellowship brings us out of the darkness and into the light. This is done when we reveal our darkness to a close friend. This is fellowship. But we keep our secrets, because we are too afraid of what would happen if we were to remove our fake masks and let everyone see us for who we really are. Our churches would benefit so much if we all would just take off our masks and be real. We would most likely not recognize each other. But real change would begin to take place.

What Does Authentic Fellowship Among Men Look Like?

Slowly but surely, Christian men are dying. Fellowship is misunderstood in many churches. I've witnessed it.

Planned fellowship within a local church tends to involve casual discussions regarding day-to-day events, some prayer time, and the study of doctrine. Are these things wrong? No. But I don't believe this is fellowship; it's too shallow. What's the point? What's the point of casual discussions? The answer is to build friendships. What's the point of prayer time? The answer is to acknowledge our dependence on God. And the point of studying doctrine is to understand who God is. I know many churches that do this on a weekly basis, yet it results in very few lives actually being changed. It's usually within these very churches that men are dropping like flies.

I don't believe folks intend to keep fellowship in its shallow state. I'm just convinced we haven't been taught the true meaning of biblical, authentic fellowship, nor have we been shown what it looks like. It is my opinion that there is a lack of authentic fellowship, and our people are suffering the consequences—especially men.

So what does this look like? Our New Testament English word *fellowship* comes from the Greek word *koinonia*. In its basic form, the word means "the act or condition of sharing something in common."[2] It is translated in various passages as contributing (giving), sharing, participation, and fellowship. So the word carries the connotation of giving to someone the thing(s) they need, whether it be experiences, undertakings, or possessions. This sounds much like agape[3] love, doesn't it?

Where in scripture does God describe this wonderful and powerful ingredient for the Church called *fellowship*? One of my favorite passages that deals with this is in 1 John 1:

> [1]**That which was from the beginning, which we have heard, which we have seen with our eyes, which we have looked upon, and our hands have handled, concerning the Word of life—**[2]**the life was manifested, and we have seen, and bear witness, and declare to you that eternal life which was with the Father and was manifested to us—**[3]**that which we have seen and heard we declare to you, that you also may have fellowship with us; and truly our fellowship is with the Father and with His Son Jesus Christ.**

The Apostle John made his point that his letter was about fellowship (I'm convinced the theme verses are 1:3-4.). This wasn't ordinary fellowship, but fellowship among him, the other apostles, and God.

Notice the pattern in verse 1: **we have heard, …seen, …looked upon, …handled.** Each word used becomes more intense. John and the other apostles had heard the life (Jesus), they had seen Him, they had looked upon Him (literally, gazed intensely), and their hands have actually touched Him. No wonder these apostles had such an intense, intimate fellowship with God! They grew closer and closer to Jesus as they spent time with Him.

Can you imagine? They watched with awe the many miracles Jesus performed. Their eyes gazed upon Him at His transfiguration. They were glued to Him at His resurrection. They touched His glorified body. They witnessed His ascension!

All the while, they grew more in love with their Savior and more connected with each other. You can't tell me in those 3½ years spent together these ordinary men weren't exposed to authenticity among each other and with Jesus where they became intensely connected emotionally, spiritually, and mentally. Yes, these men grew to love Jesus and to love each other.

Can you imagine being one of the disciples? Picture this in your mind: It is an early, cool morning and the other guys are still trying to wake up. Peter is cooking breakfast over an open flame. It's fish… again. James and John are arguing over something petty, as brothers tend to do.

You go to the river to wash your face, and when you get up you see Jesus sitting right next to you. He speaks, "Good morning!" You respond with a smile, "Good morning, Jesus."

He says, "So I realize that you had an interesting dream last night." Your smile immediately leaves as your face turns all shades of red, while you recall the dream of that certain young lady you saw yesterday in the marketplace. She was gorgeous! You didn't just see her, your eyes *gazed* upon her. Now, with the Lord sitting beside you, you feel embarrassed and heartbroken that you sinned against Him. The only thing you feel like doing now is hiding underneath a rock. But then Jesus smiles and says, "Come here. I want to show you something."

The two of you walk over to the rest of the men who are sitting down around the fire for their morning meal. Jesus sits down, and you sit next to Him. He proclaims, "Hey guys, our brother had a dream last night about that good-looking lady we all saw at the marketplace."

You prepare for the punishment and condemnation. But instead, you hear Peter speak up while flipping the fish patties, "Yup, I saw her. I admit it—I looked twice." Then James leans in toward the fire and speaks up, "Yeah, I saw John take a good look!" John gives his brother an elbow in the ribs. Andrew chimes in, "I saw her, but I was able to keep moving forward. No lust here!"

Then Jesus brings it home. "Brothers, remember what I told you about lusting after another woman? It's like committing adultery in your heart. But your honesty is good for your heart, and confession bonds us together."

By this time, you don't feel alone. Jesus turns to you and raises His eyebrows. A smile slowly forms on His face as He looks straight into your eyes. Your heartbeat settles back down, and you say to the King of kings, "My Lord, I confess that I lusted after that lady yesterday. Forgive me." Jesus puts His right arm around your shoulders and responds, "Whoever confesses and forsakes His sins will receive mercy." You know you've been forgiven!

The color in your face returns to normal, and you feel as though your brothers are standing side-by-side with you, even in the mental battles you face. The other disciples who shared in your sin follow suit as they see how you have been forgiven by Jesus. You feel His unrelenting love for you as He pulls you close to His side and laughs with the other guys at the honesty that just took place.

You know that your Savior is before you as your Faithful Leader and behind you as your Strong Support. Actually, He's sitting right next to you. He hasn't left you there by yourself to wallow in your guilt. You're forgiven. What camaraderie! What unique fellowship! This kind of fellowship should still occur today. Jesus is still the Head of the Church.

I've talked with so many men who have shared their burdens with me. For many of them, it was difficult to open up and become vulnerable. However, several times I have asked them how they felt after they talked openly with me about their struggles. Every one of them told me the same thing: They felt freedom. They felt like a weight had been lifted off their shoulders. This is precisely why many Christian men who are deep into their secret sins actually want to get caught. It's because the weight is too much to bear alone. The truth, is authentic fellowship is liberating.

The principle I get out of this pattern in 1 John is that biblical fellowship among men includes becoming real with brothers with whom we already have a relationship. And, together, we grow closer to our Father with whom we all have a relationship. There is the aspect of quality time spent with other brothers while being authentic, loyal, and committed to each other. The purpose of this time is to *give* to one another, *share* with one another, and *participate* in the lives of one another.

Yet notice in verse 3 that John uses only two of the four words from verse 1: **seen** and **heard**. He leaves out **looked upon** and **handled**. Perhaps he is saying, "Trust what I am saying…we know real fellowship! We wish you could have *gazed upon Jesus* and actually *touched Him* like we have, but we want to declare to you what we have **seen** and **heard** from Him so that you can experience deep, intimate fellowship with us and with Him."

Only the disciples spent time with Jesus, i.e., gazed intensely upon Him. Only the disciples were close enough and intimate enough to touch Him. I can only imagine that when John wrote that part he was picturing in his mind the time when he laid his head on the chest of His Messiah at the dinner table. No one can explain moments like that. No one else had experiences like these—only John and the other disciples. They certainly understood authentic fellowship.

His point is not that we can't experience intimate fellowship with Jesus, because when Jesus ascended to heaven He sent His Spirit to dwell within each believer. God dwelling in me is a unique and unfathomable sense of fellowship. Truly, we have an amazing God Who would do something so loving and gracious as this. He would even send His only Son to be the sacrifice for my sins so I can have fellowship with Him.

I believe John experienced biblical fellowship with Jesus because Jesus made it His *priority* to get into the lives of John and the other disciples. Fellowship takes initiative. It's only real when one understands that Church is people because it makes people a priority. Biblical fellowship is entering the life of another, and this allows our fellowship with God to become more intense, as well. 1 John 4:9-10 describes what the love of God is like.

> **⁹In this the love of God was manifested toward us, that God has sent His only begotten Son into the world, that we might live through Him. ¹⁰In this is love, not that we loved God, but that He loved us and sent His Son to be the propitiation for our sins.**

That's initiative. That's love. That's God. He didn't wait for us to come to Him, His Love came to us, and this Love was and is embodied in the Person of Jesus Christ. Now, take a look at the next two verses John writes:

> **¹¹Beloved, if God so loved us, we also ought to love one another. ¹²No one has seen God at any time. If we love one another, God abides in us, and His love has been perfected in us.**

Did you catch that? We ought to love one another with this kind of love. Remember, this kind of love takes initiative. It's a priority!

Here's the clincher: God abides in us *as we love one another.* That word *abides* means *fellowship.* In other words, I enter into deep, intimate fellowship with God as I enter into deep, intimate fellowship with others. I cannot be in fellowship with God when I'm out of fellowship with my brothers.

And according to John, fellowship is made of love. They're inseparable. They go hand-in-hand. Paul defines this love in 1 Corinthians 13:4-8a by using sixteen different descriptions. Love is not shallow, nor is it easily defined. John described it by mentioning one Man's name: Jesus.

Love is fellowship with Jesus and with others, and it is intended to be deep. Fellowship is shallow when there is a lack of love. Our churches experience shallow fellowship (or none at all) because there is a lack of this kind of love which John speaks of in his epistle. We will spend more time on this in Chapter 4, but to put it simply: Know love? Know fellowship. No love? No fellowship.

I'm Not that Kind of Person

You may be thinking, "But I don't need that kind of relationship with other guys. I'm fine just as I am. It's just not my personality." May I suggest all Christian men crave true, biblical fellowship? I'm one of them, and I'm convinced you are, too. The truth is, we were created for fellowship. It's programmed in our DNA. Did you know research has found that prolonged loneliness can actually affect us physically?

Check this out:

- At Ohio State University College of Medicine, scientists found that patients who scored above average in loneliness had significantly poorer functioning of their immune systems.
- In Sweden, a ten-year study of 150 middle-aged men found that social isolation was one of the best predictors of mortality.
- A report published in the journal *Science* said that social isolation is as significant to mortality rates as smoking, high blood pressure, high cholesterol, obesity, and lack of physical exercise. In fact, when age is adjusted for, social isolation is as great or greater a mortality risk than smoking.
- At Stanford University School of Medicine, Dr. David Spiegel conducted research in which patients with metastatic breast cancer were randomly divided into two groups. One group received the usual medical care, while the other received the usual care plus weekly ninety-minute support group meetings for one year.

Although he planned the study expecting there would be no difference in life span between the two groups, five years later he found that the patients who attended the weekly group support meetings had twice the survival rate of the other group.[4]

All people need friends. All believers need one another. We need fellowship. The Christian life is not intended to be lived with shallow relationships with other believers, just as it is not intended to be lived with a shallow relationship with God.

Biblical fellowship is not shallow. It's deep and personal. It's on the emotional level and the spiritual level. It requires time, selflessness, energy, initiative, honesty, authenticity, loyalty, trust, and commitment. No one possesses all of these characteristics naturally, which is why many of us never experience true fellowship. Those who miss out on it are not experiencing the life that God intends for us to live.

The passages we've been looking at teach that every believer—man, woman, boy, and girl—has the commandment to enter into each other's world and love one another there. For men, our society tries to dictate that a real man is one who doesn't need anyone else.

You know what I mean. Who hasn't wished he was more like John Wayne, Clint Eastwood, John Rambo, or Arnold How-do-you-spell-his-last-name? However, I'm convinced that true fellowship carries the potential to keep us from giving in to temptation.

I know too many brothers who have fallen because they have not experienced this thing called fellowship. They thought they could handle their temptations alone. Later, they felt they *had* to handle it alone. It is my opinion that when we grasp the fact that ministry is people, we will pursue biblical fellowship.

I think fellowship motivates men to be a part of church life. It gives them a connection, a sense of belonging and acceptance, and it brings healing, warmth, depth, and wholeness to individuals within the body. And it brings unity. Biblical fellowship is not passive, but active. It takes initiative.

If Bob is an uninvolved member of his church, George doesn't wait for Bob to come to him for fellowship, George goes to Bob. The love of Christ takes initiative. His Spirit living inside each believer gives the power and passion to share His love. God's love is fellowship, and biblical fellowship involves both horizontal and vertical aspects: loving others and loving God.

CHAPTER THREE

FREEDOM COMES FROM SHARING CHRIST'S PASSION

I love going to the movies. I love action movies and comedy movies, but not romance or scary movies. But I love taking my wife to see a scary movie. When we see a scary movie together, I'll wrap my arms around her, not to keep her from being scared but because *I'm* terrified! I know—it's usually the other way around. Go ahead and call me a wimp; I can take it.

The best movies, though, are the ones where people applaud at the end. But the movie that probably moved the world more than any other received no applause at the end. I saw this movie, too. I remember sitting between my dad and my brother as the ending credits rolled up the screen. The movie was over, but not a single person was leaving. Most were crying. Many were staring at the screen, and only a few whispers could be heard.

The atmosphere in the theater created by this movie was like none I had ever felt before. I had seen many movies depicting the crucifixion of Christ, but Mel Gibson's *The Passion of the Christ* had done it. This movie drove every viewer to an extremity of emotion. It either made people throughout the world become more in love with the Savior or become angry with Christianity. One of the biggest ways this movie impacted me was by making me aware of just how passionate Jesus was (and is) for people. I guess that's why they call it *The Passion of the Christ.*

In His obedience to the Father, Jesus died for people. Today His body on earth is made up of people. To the glory of the Father, which is our highest goal, the bottom line for the Church is people. Plain and simple. And when we men wrap our minds around this fact, I believe we will pursue authentic fellowship with each other. To put it another way, authentic fellowship requires the priority of glorifying the Father by developing a passion for people.

The Reason

Let me ask you a question. What do you think about the word *passion*? I love that word. Are you passionate about anything? What drives you? What makes you tick? Why do you do the things you do? Is it out of sheer will? Out of discipline? Because you're afraid no one else will do it?

What about love? Motivation towards holiness? Motivation towards Christlikeness? Are you passionate for Christ? Can you see how unusually passionate He was for people during His ministry on earth? I think Jesus was an extremist when it comes to being passionate for people. I believe there was a driving love that motivated Him to do the things He did: heal, preach, forgive, change lives, even die.

I've often wondered if I can have that same passion, that same love. Can I be passionate about the Savior so much as to be a reflection of His love to others even when people hurt me? Certainly I can't deny the pain associated with being let down or feeling betrayed, and neither could Jesus. But it didn't take away His passion. People are at the top of His love list. I think Jesus' motto has something to do with being passionate for people. I think that drives Him. How ironic—that same thing by which Jesus was passionately driven, namely His love for His Father and for people, drove Him to the cross. Why? Because He wanted it that way. Because He was passionate for people.

It gets better. People are His passion, but not His *greatest* passion. His *greatest* passion is to accomplish the will of His Father (Lk. 2:49,

22:42; Jn. 9:4). And since it was the Father's will for Jesus to come and seek and save that which was lost, then people are the Father's passion as well. In other words, Jesus' passion for people is doubled because His Father is passionate for people through Him. You are incredibly loved by God!

But people hurt people. They break promises, slander, gossip, and so on. To us, people can sometimes be a real pain. However, to Him, people are precious. Oh, and I am a person. I break promises, slander, and gossip. I try not to, but I know I'm still precious to Jesus. We, sinners, are precious to Him because He is passionate for people. I really want that kind of passion for God and for people. I want to be driven that way.

I must admit something. Many times I'm passionate about only one person: me. And when I am this way, I shy away from pursuing fellowship with other guys because even Christian men can break promises, slander, and gossip. (That's right, guys, it's not just the ladies!)

But according to 1 John, if I'm not experiencing true fellowship with God's people, then this affects my fellowship with God. And my fellowship with God affects my being a partaker of Christ. Remember, a *metochoi*.

The Proof

I love the following passage from Matthew 9:

> **35And Jesus went about all the cities and villages, teaching in their synagogues, preaching the gospel of the kingdom, and healing every sickness and every disease among the people. 36But when He saw the multitudes, He was moved with compassion for them, because they were harassed and scattered, like sheep having no shepherd.**

In verse 35, Jesus is healing the sick, teaching, and evangelizing throughout the land. It's verse 36 that brings chills to my spine. "But when He saw the multitudes, He was moved with compassion for them because they were harassed and scattered, like sheep having no shepherd." What was Matthew saying about the people? He was equating people to sheep. I resemble that remark because sheep are easily confused. Quite frankly, they're stupid. Really stupid.

Let's say a flock of sheep are grazing in a meadow near a cliff. The shepherd, being overcome by some sort of depression, decides to end his life by throwing himself over the cliff, falling to the bottom and creating a mess on the ground below. Now, I've been told every one of his sheep would proceed to toss itself over the edge of the cliff, falling to the bottom and creating an even larger mess on the ground below. They do this because they follow their leader everywhere he goes.

This may sound crazy. Surely you would never do something like that. Maybe, but before we get too proud thinking we're much smarter, let me remind you that God compares us to sheep. We, too, are easily confused and stupid. So stupid, in fact, that we follow the progression of many other Christian men by falling into the same destructive behaviors that have led them to their own destruction. We have seen their death, and we still follow.

Despite this, we are so precious that God sent His only Son to die for us. We are so precious that He sent His Holy Spirit to comfort us, convict us, fill us, and strengthen us. We are so precious that Jesus is coming back to bring us to be with Him for eternity! We are so precious that Jesus was moved with compassion in Matthew 9. In fact, because of this compassion, Jesus was motivated to commission His disciples in Chapter 10. But He waited until they saw how compassionate He was for people.

Compassion can be defined as a feeling of deep sympathy and sorrow for someone struck by misfortune, accompanied by a desire to alleviate the suffering. Sounds much like mercy to me.

This is the feeling that overcame Jesus when He saw that the people were harassed and scattered by false teachings. They were confused. Just like sheep with no shepherd, they had no protection from the ravaging wolves. To say the least, they were struck by misfortune. The Pharisees were supposed to be their spiritual leaders, their shepherds. But instead of feeding their flock, they used their positions for their own gain.

The shepherds strove to take care of themselves rather than their sheep. When the ravaging wolves came, the shepherds ran, leaving their poor sheep alone—harassed, scattered, dead. They were hirelings. The sheep didn't belong to them, so why would they sacrifice their lives for a bunch of stupid sheep? They were cowards. They deserted their flock when the wolves came near. Shame on those Pharisees.

The Plea

The Pharisees viewed the people as wretched sinners. They were disgusting in their shepherds' sight. However, Jesus viewed them as hurting and depressed—torn down and laid waste. The sight of these harassed and scattered people tore His heart in two. It charged His emotions the moment He laid eyes on them. He was moved with compassion. He not only came to sacrifice His body but also His reputation. He didn't care what the spiritual leaders of the Israelites thought of Him when He was seen with the unrighteous of the land. He hung around them not because He was participating in their lifestyles, but because He had compassion for them.

As Christians, we are often so worried about our reputations that we avoid helping those who are hurting, depressed, without hope, without peace, without love. Too many pastors are more concerned about their own careers and needs than about caring for their flock. This is perverted! We are called to love those that are hated. We are called to care for those that are weak. We are called to be a compassionate people, willing to change the world. But our churches must change first.

Can you imagine what the disciples thought when they saw the Messiah break? Jesus was emotionally overcome. I can just see Him falling apart before Peter, James, John, Andrew, and the others. I can just see the men looking at each other and wondering what was going on. Then, they heard His words,

³⁷...The harvest truly is plentiful, but the laborers are few. ³⁸Therefore pray the Lord of the harvest to send out laborers into His harvest.

The harvest to which Jesus was referring was apparently lost Jewish people who had come to hear Him. What a plea from the Savior for us to pray to the Father to send out laborers to spread the good news of salvation!

Yet there is another principle we can take from this passage. It shows the compassion that Jesus has for people, doesn't it? Guys, underline the next three sentences. There is a vast harvest in our churches today. A big part of this harvest contains Christian men who are on the road to destruction. We need laborers who are as compassionate as Jesus is—compassionate enough to enter the world of these men and offer them hope, peace, and direction, and help them see the way out of their darkness.

The Church needs laborers who have removed their fake masks and let others see them for who they really are—warts and all. For we are all stupid, but even in our stupidity, *we are all precious!* Christian men must see one another for who we really are. We must bring up the obvious and deal with it. But it begins with you. Someone in your church needs to champion this cause. Someone needs to be passionate about people like Jesus is and begin this phenomenal thing called fellowship.

A Few Hindrances

Authentic fellowship requires the priority to glorify the Father by developing a passion for people, but many times churches may unintentionally (or sadly, sometimes intentionally) cause a few hindrances that will prevent authentic fellowship from ever happening.

Most of these hindrances are not wrong in themselves but are used in wrong ways. They are good things that become bad because of the priority given to them within the church. In other words, they become the *end* instead of the *means to the end*. The *end* should be to glorify the Father by being passionate for people. Yet many common things become the *end*, and the truth of the matter is that anything within the Church can become a hindrance—politics, building programs, ministry programs, and music, just to name a few.

What is the reason for this? Why are there hindrances to authentic fellowship? You'll love my answer. The answer is because the Church is people. You read that right. Seems ironic? When God's people fail to realize their purpose for existing, which involves glorifying the Father by being passionate for one another, we put something else in its place. When a church does this, it is at this precise moment that it fails the Head, Jesus Christ. The failure is placing as the *end* anything other than glorifying the Father by being passionate for people.

Perhaps you've been in a situation where you've witnessed right things being given wrong priority. Maybe you've even suffered or seen someone else suffer because of it. Here are a couple of situations that can cause a hindrance to authentic fellowship.

Church politics. Reading those two words together usually causes severe headaches for most pastors. Some would say they are an oxymoron. Due to the secular world's tainting the word *politics*, most people cringe when they hear it.

Here is the best definition for *politics* I've ever heard. Someone once said *poli-* means *many*, and *-tics* are *blood-sucking pests*. That's sounds a little tainted, albeit true in many cases. Perhaps that's why people cringe when they hear the word.

Politics is a dirty word nowadays. Unfortunately, politics are often dirty in many churches. But politics is actually none other than implementing policies, rules, and regulations, which are definitely needed in all organizations, especially the Church. Yet when they become the *end* and not the *means to the end*, people are run over and God is not glorified.

Rules and regulations can definitely be a hindrance when they are seen as the *end* and not as the *means to an end*. Once my wife and I were in a small group with leaders who were an older married couple. They were loving, caring folks who earnestly desired fellowship. However, the husband had a hindrance that prevented him from expressing a true passion for people. Under his leadership, there was a central purpose that was foundational to his philosophy for small groups. Perhaps he had good intentions (fellowship, intimacy, Bible study, prayer), but his philosophy was poor due to the hindrance of politics.

He was passionate about politics. He wrote up a set of guidelines with rules and regulations that the members of the small group had to sign in order to be approved as part of the group, and if any member broke any rule, he could be eliminated from the group.

For example, it was clear he wanted the group to be committed to the time they were to meet, which was evident in the guidelines (i.e., don't be late, don't leave early, don't miss except for sickness, etc). If someone could not be committed to that time, then he was not committed to the group as a whole and, therefore, should be eliminated from the group.

Perhaps he could have taught the group to be committed to each other, rather than to any guidelines. Being committed to each other requires the fruit of the Spirit, while being committed to rules and regulations requires a pencil and paper.

The leaders of this small group saw the need for people to be committed and wanted to teach their group to be committed so they could build better relationships. Yet he misunderstood the right method of that teaching. He had a structured and organized mind. However, this structure needed to be balanced with grace in order for authentic fellowship to exist.

The key ingredient in the New Testament is grace. Grace is freedom. It has freed me from the penalty of sin. It continually frees me from the power of sin when I submit to the Spirit, and it will free me from the presence of sin. Yet freedom is risky. I am free to live as I please. At the time of my justification, God did not make me sign or force me to adhere to guidelines that dictate what I promise not to do (curse, lust, covet, etc.). I am free to sin, just as I am free to live in obedience.

However, there are consequences to my sin. If I choose sin, it leads to death. If I choose obedience, it leads to my abundant life (Rom. 6:15-23). I am free to choose. I am free to die, but I am also free to live the abundant life that God desires for me.

My point is that God has the Christian life set up in freedom. I am free to go to church. I am free to stay home. I am free to make my own priorities. I am free to be committed to something or not be committed to something. I am even free to commit to something and not follow through. Freedom doesn't mean I will always choose the right thing, but God saw freedom (grace) as a much better way to live than the confines of the law. If I live by the law only, then I focus on my outward self (i.e., the Israelites). Yet if I live by grace (freedom), then I can inwardly choose the right thing if my spirit is in tune with the Holy Spirit.

Grace has freed me to listen to and follow the leading of the Holy Spirit. Therefore, who am I to say that any person missing my small group because he has had a rough week and needs rest is unacceptable? Perhaps he was led by the Spirit to do so.

Authentic fellowship in small groups is needed, but authentic fellowship within the family is essential. We teach that the family is God's first institution, and that which Satan is striving to destroy. We believe parents should spend quality and quantity time with their children. If a father has had to work double time for the last few weeks and the wife has been the one at home with the kids many nights throughout the week, should we demand that he come to our small group even when he desperately needs to spend time with his children, or should we give him the freedom to make the right decision? Should we cut him out of the group, eliminating that fellowship because he has chosen to spend some time with his family—a necessity taught by the Scriptures?

I understand the need for structure and am not the opponent of it. God is a God of order, not chaos, so I'm not suggesting that grace means a chaotic way of ministering to people. However, perhaps it is wrong to force a group of people to follow certain rules that will eliminate the relational aspect of the group.[5] Telling a couple they are not part of our group because they cannot commit to the time of the meeting is, in my opinion, not realizing Christ's passion for people.

Sure, we need rules and regulations, but they are to be treated as a means to the end. Otherwise, people are not the bottom line. God is not glorified in His Church. Church politics are glorified. Rules and regulations are the bottom line.

Stuck to Programs. Having spent thirteen years as a youth pastor, I see the need for well-run programs. Yet I remember the day when it occurred to our youth leadership team how severely unbalanced our successful youth ministry had become when it came to our programs. Our group was growing in number, and many people were joining our church because of the youth ministry we had. But God had been developing in us a hunger that our ministry was just not filling—fellowship and evangelism—and we wanted to implement these two things in my youth ministry.

The Lord used a series of sermons and skits we did to spark the interest throughout our church for deeper fellowship and evangelism. The church leaders recognized that we had not emphasized either of these at all in any of our ministries. We had been driven to study the doctrines of God's Word, but we had not provided the venues to learn how and where to apply these doctrines.

Soon everyone became excited over the new direction of becoming a "one another" and "evangelistic-minded" church. However, it wasn't long until we ran into a large, solid brick wall. That wall was made entirely of all the other programs we had already established in our church, and no one wanted to get rid of a single brick. Almost all of these programs had to do with studying God's Word.

I was curious to know how much time we were spending on the programs we already had in place, so we worked up a chart. We had come to the understanding of what God really wanted from His Church: to love Him, to love one another, and to reach the lost. Another way of stating this is studying His Word, fellowshipping with one another, and sharing the gospel. So we made a chart of all the weekly programs our church had for our people. We put those three items as headings at the top of the chart and listed our programs under the appropriate category.

When we finished, we were rather astonished. We were expecting our people to be involved in approximately twenty hours of ministry each week. And do you know what category received the majority of those programs? It was *studying His Word*.

The problem was that we had left no time for our people to fellowship with one another or to share the gospel. We had not provided the venue for our people to put into practice what was being taught in Sunday school, from behind the pulpit, at midweek Bible studies, and more. Something had to give, but no one wanted to give up any of the programs that were already established.

The church desperately needed two things: to actively engage in biblical fellowship and to obey the command to evangelize. Sure, we need programs, but programs can hinder authentic fellowship in any church. This happens when programs become the *end* instead of the *means to the end*. We felt that we needed these programs in order to attract people, and keep people, and because other churches had these. I'm not saying these programs were bad; nor am I saying that God didn't use these programs for good. Yet many of the programs in our church seemed to cause an unbalanced philosophy of ministry. The result was that we had little to no fellowship, and we didn't evangelize at all.

A wise man once said, "If you always do what you've always done, you'll always get what you've always got." My dad often asks me, "Son, how's your walk with God?" I know my answer depends on my fellowship with God and others.

I'll ask you a question. How's it working for you? How deep is your fellowship with God? How deep is your fellowship with others? Are you passionate for obedience to the Father? Are you passionate for people—His people?

I'm convinced that, in general, Christian men are being less effective as real leaders in our homes and churches. I'm convinced the reason for this is because Christian men are missing out on authentic fellowship. We miss out because we aren't taught and challenged to become passionate for people. Men need to get into the lives of each other. We need to know we all struggle with the same things—to differing degrees, but the same struggles. We need to take off our masks—they're fake anyway—and declare the obvious: We screw up and need each other to remain focused. We need to be committed to each other. We need fellowship, for without it, we die.

Jesus is passionate for people. So should we be.

CHAPTER FOUR

FREEDOM COMES FROM TWO INGREDIENTS

Nothing great happens on its own. Success takes work—team work. NFL football teams don't win the Super Bowl by just showing up and giving mediocre effort. Great armies have never won difficult battles without carefully drawn up battle plans. And authentic fellowship among Christian men in our churches simply will not happen unless we work together toward this common goal.

But first, we must take a good, hard look at what Scripture tells us are key ingredients to this phenomenon called *fellowship*. I want to share with you two such ingredients throughout the pages of this chapter. Then we will draw up some battle plans that can keep us victorious on the front lines.

Obey the Father: Love One Another

I have been to a few churches that seemed to be lifeless. They tried to go places, but nothing ever happened. Ideas for the future were brought up and thrown out. Sometimes people came in the front door, but others were fleeing out of the back. It is hard to see churches suffocate.

One common denominator among them all, at least one that I have noticed, is that the people that made up each church really didn't *know* each other. And I'm convinced that many of them really didn't *know* God, either. Before you call me harsh and judgmental, I must tell you what I mean by the word *know*.

As I stated earlier, 1 John is about fellowship (1:3-4) with God and with one another. John made known to us that perhaps our most intimate moments of fellowship with God occur when we are experiencing deep fellowship with other believers (4:9-12). John states, also, that sin breaks fellowship with God. It doesn't remove our relationship with Him, but it does put a wedge in our fellowship with Him. Here, again, is the Apostle John (1 John 2):

> **³Now by this we know that we know Him, if we keep His commandments. ⁴He who says, "I know Him," and does not keep His commandments, is a liar, and the truth is not in him. ⁵But whoever keeps His word, truly the love of God is perfected in him. By this we know that we are in Him.**

A teenage boy once asked his dad, who was lounging in his recliner after a wonderful meal, "Dad, how do I know if I'm in love?" His dad answered, "Son, you just know." The boy walked into the kitchen where his mom was washing the dishes that were just used for their dinner. He asked, "Mom, how do I know if I'm in love?" His mom, still scrubbing the pot in her hand, replied, "I have no idea, son. Why don't you go ask your father?"

Apparently, Mom wasn't feeling the love. I guess we could say the fellowship between Mom and Dad was broken. How do we know we are in fellowship? Fellowship with God involves fellowship with one another. Sin (which usually involves one another) breaks my fellowship with God. And fellowship with one another is one of the things that can keep me from sin because I am supported, encouraged, and prayed for, and my burdens are not carried alone.

This passage in 1 John sounds a little weird, I must admit. "We know that we know?" What does that mean? Actually, these are two different tenses of the same word for *know*. Our English language doesn't always bring out all the tenses of the Greek. The first *know* (in the present tense) indicates a realization, while the second *know* (in the perfect tense) carries a more meaningful value, like an intense intimacy.

Since John is talking about fellowship, and this context in Chapter 2 is dealing with sin, we can translate this verse like this: "Here is how we *realize* that we are having *deep, intimate fellowship* with God. It's by obeying His commandments."

Remember the Israelites? Those were the folks in the Old Testament whom God had chosen as a special people through which the line of the Messiah would come. The Israelites sinned a lot, and when they did, God's blessing was removed from them. In fact, they were cursed, as God told them they would be if they sinned against Him. And, boy, did they know how to sin.

When they sinned, the Israelites were afflicted by the surrounding enemies. When they cried out in repentance, God sent a judge to deliver them, which made them happy. But after a while they sinned again and were afflicted again, and they cried out again in repentance. So guess what God did? He sent another judge to deliver them yet again. This cycle was repeated by the Israelites twelve times. (Read Judges. It's all there!) One would think they would have learned to turn from their sin, but instead they learned how merciful God is. What was happening was *the community of the Israelites kept being disrupted by their sin, and God dealt with them as He saw fit.*

In Joshua 7, we read of a time when Joshua, the leader of Israel whom God had appointed to lead the nation into the promised land of Canaan, led the mighty Israelite warriors into battle, only to see them utterly conquered. When Joshua asked God why, God said it was because there was sin in the camp. *The progression of their community was disrupted by their sin, and God dealt with them as He saw fit.*

In Acts 5, we read of another time when a married couple brought money to the Apostles to be given to those in need in the new Church. They had sold some land and kept some of the money for themselves, but they told the Apostles they were giving *all* of the proceeds to the Church. Peter told them Satan had filled their hearts so that they had lied to the Holy Spirit. They died on the spot. *The community of the new Church was disrupted by their sin, and God dealt with them as He saw fit.*

In 1 Corinthians 11, the Apostle Paul told the church in Corinth that some of them had died because they were abusing the Lord's Supper. Once again, *the community of that church was disrupted by their sin, and God dealt with them as He saw fit.*

So this has me wondering if it could be that God will not bless a local church when its community is disrupted by the sins of its members. I really think so. What is His blessing, anyway? I believe it is the fulfillment of His purpose for His Church: to populate heaven, to enjoy His peace and bounty, to thrive in the abundant life of walking in the Spirit, to produce fruit, to live by the fruit of the Spirit, to enjoy the unity of the body, to grow in number and in grace, to know God more fully. All of this is to the glory of God.

Could it be that God withholds these blessings because of sin in the camp? There is no abundant life when we are in sin. There is no unity of the body when we are in sin. There is no fruit when we are in sin. And we are not *knowing* God when we are in sin. I mean really *knowing* God. In other words, we cannot have fellowship with God when we are in sin. And we cannot have fellowship with God when we are not in fellowship with each other.

What's really interesting is the one commandment that John emphasizes in Chapter 2 directly after the passage mentioned above: *love your brother.*

> **[8]Again, a new commandment I write to you... [9]He who says he is in the light, and hates his brother, is in darkness until now. [10]He who loves his brother abides in the light, and there is no cause for stumbling in him. [11]But he who hates his brother is in darkness and walks in darkness, and does not know where he is going, because the darkness has blinded his eyes.**

When I do not love my brother, I'm out of fellowship with God. Plain and simple. Why would He bless that? When a church contains folks who do not love one another, the church is not experiencing the fellowship that God intends and in which He delights. Why would He bless that church? Perhaps He is standing at their front door knocking, desiring to come in and have fellowship with them.

Knowing...love...fellowship. Are you beginning to see the connection here? If *knowing* is intimate fellowship, and *love* is intimate fellowship, and we really don't *know* one another at my church, then we really aren't *loving* one another at my church. Let's talk about this love again by revisiting 1 John 4:9-10 and taking a deeper look:

> **⁹In this the love of God was manifested toward us, that God has sent His only begotten Son into the world, that we might live through Him. ¹⁰In this is love, not that we loved God, but that He loved us and sent His Son to be the propitiation for our sins.**

Of all the passages in the Bible that proclaim the greatness of God's love for us, this one brings me the most pleasure. In his commentary on 1 John, called *Maximum Joy*, David Anderson brings this passage to life by observing four things about God's love.

First, John says this love was manifested toward us. It was given to us. All of it! This love is *all-giving*. Second, he describes this love in the Person of Jesus as the One who was sent. Jesus was the ultimate sacrifice for the sins of the world. This love is *sacrificial*. Third, John tells us because of this love Jesus was sent into the world. The world does not deserve this love. We deserve Hell. However, God so loved the world that He gave His only begotten Son! This loves is *directed toward people who do not deserve it*. And last, God did not wait for us to love Him in order for us to receive His love. God loved us first. This love *takes first initiative*. So this love is all-giving, it is sacrificial, it is directed toward people who don't deserve it, and it takes the first initiative.

I love how God loves me! Knowing how stupid I can act as His child, I also know how precious I am. I am deeply loved. But here's the loaded question: Do I love people with this kind of love? Do you love the people in your church with this kind of love? John says we are to love our brothers. Paul said this over and over again: love one another. This is obeying His commandments. And this is how we know that we *know* Him—by *knowing* one another. This is how we fellowship with Him. It's by loving one another. This is how we are authentic.

So, as men, are you showing this kind of love for other guys in your church, or are you just showing up and putting forth mediocre effort? Do you see the vital connection between fellowship with God and fellowship with others? Indeed, the two are inseparable!

The truth is that we are mostly acquaintances in our churches, but I'm convinced that in order for true fellowship to exist we must follow in obedience to our Father and love one another. We love one another by entering each other's world. I can't sacrifice for you if I don't know what to sacrifice for. I can't give to you if I don't know that you have need. I can't love you if I don't get to know you.

As men, we must move in our relationships with one another from acquaintances to deep, loyal, and committed friendships. This takes time, effort, and patience on our part, but we will be rewarded greatly from this God-given gift of fellowship. In order to do this, let's look at the second key ingredient that most Christians tend to overlook. Most people avoid this next one like the plague.

Confess Your Sins to One Another

Fellowship is deep, not shallow. Biblical fellowship is authentic, not fake. But men are usually too afraid to be authentic—far too fearful to ever confess to each other. Yes, in order for fellowship among men to be authentic, the Bible tells us to confess our sins to one another. I'm afraid of that. But according to Scripture fears can be overcome.

I've been skydiving twice in my lifetime, and I plan to go many more times! I've got to tell you about my first experience. I called the skydive place to set reservations and was told to arrive before 9 a.m. to get our place in line. We were so excited! Oh, I wasn't about to go alone. Although the thought of jumping out of a plane at 14,000 feet was extremely fascinating, it was also very terrifying, so

I encouraged a few of my friends to join me. We were all terrified, but the guys at the skydive facility were professionals, and we trusted their abilities and talents.

My friends and I arrived at Skydive Houston in Waller, Texas, on a Saturday morning at 8 a.m., but no one was there. We walked around to find someone—anyone. Finally, I saw a hangar with the door cracked open and a radio blaring. I peeked in to see a young man working out in what appeared to be his living quarters, and I had to yell over the radio to get his attention.

In a strong South African accent, he told me I should just hang around for a while until the other employees showed up. After a while a couple of professionals arrived. Nervously, we hung around for three hours, during which time we had to watch a video in which a man who sported a 3-foot-long beard and never left the 70's told us about how he had invented the tandem-style jump. (That means jumping with a professional buckled to your back.)

After watching the video, I spent 30 minutes of my life which I'll never get back signing a one-inch stack of papers in which every other word or phrase was either "death," "liability," or "we are not responsible." I didn't read it all; I just kept signing my name.

Finally, it was time to board the plane, but we were told the plane they usually use broke down the day before, so we had to use the "other" plane. I think it was a Cessna; but whatever it was, it was definitely small. With the pilot, three jumpers, and three professionals inside that small plane, it was very tight. As the plane cork-screwed its way up to 14,000 feet, the pros began to buckle themselves to our backs. So this 45-year-old guy told me to squat with my back to his front. I did as I was told, and he latched six or so buckles, which pulled me in nice and snug to his chest.

When he finished, we were not at 14,000 feet quite yet, so we just had to sit there and wait. I sat in his lap. Nice and snug. I began to wonder what else I had signed my name to back on the ground. Perhaps I should've read it all.

Then the door opened and a rush of cool air blew in. It was invigorating! We were officially at 14,000 feet, and we (my man and I) were first in line to maneuver to the door and make our jump. In order to do so inside such a small plane, I had to walk on my knees. Remember, I had some man chained to my back. Are you picturing what this looks like in your mind? My heart was pounding, and my nerves were shot! I couldn't believe what I was doing! I didn't know what I feared more—what was before me or what was behind me. But we made our way to the door, and he counted...*1*...*2*...I was going with him, whether I liked it or not...*3!*

Now because we were not in the usual plane, but a much smaller and slower one, we didn't catch the wind like we were supposed to. In other words, we weren't sky *diving*; it was more like sky *rolling*. All I remember seeing was earth, plane, earth, plane, earth, plane; and each time, the earth got bigger while the plane got smaller. After a few flips at three miles high in the sky, we finally caught our balance, but I did not realize until we got to the ground that we were *not* supposed to be flipping!

It was the most thrilling ride of my life. Falling at a rate of 120 miles per hour for one solid minute, I couldn't hear myself scream. Then he pulled the chute and all was quiet and peaceful. I took out my cell phone (I had kept it in a special pouch), held it carefully (we were still 4,000 feet above the earth), and called my wife, who had refused to come and watch. She asked me if I was on my way home. I smiled and said, "Yes."

Skydiving used to be a fear of mine. I overcame it. When I looked out the door of that airplane and saw the earth far below, I was petrified. I could hardly move, but I overcame it. I believe I overcame it because I had someone with me, buckled firmly to my back, who had successfully completed more than 4,500 jumps. So I wasn't alone. I also had my friends with me to encourage me onward. They were encouraging because they were jumping, too. We did it together! And I can't wait to do it again.

All it took was that first jump, and I was hooked. But we men allow fear to overcome us. Men are cowards when it comes to fellowship because one of the key ingredients to biblical fellowship among men—one that makes it authentic—is confession. We look into this idea of confession in James 5, and we are petrified. Yet the fact is, we have a Professional with us. He's got our backs. He's our Advocate, and He's already paid for the sin we need to confess. And confess we should—both to God and to others. After all, our friends go jumping off into the same kinds of sins from time to time, anyway. So we're in this together.

Let's take a look at this passage in James 5:

> **¹⁶Confess your trespasses to one another, and pray for one another, that you may be healed. The effective, fervent prayer of a righteous man avails much.**

In this context, James' main thought is the subject of *prayer*. In verse 13, James encourages a believer who is struggling with life issues to pray. In verse 14, he instructs the sick (or better, "weary") Christian to call for the elders to pray over him in order for him to be healed. In verse 15, James connects the idea of sin as being related to the believer's sickness. He doesn't indicate that all sicknesses are due to sin, but if the believer has sinned, he could be forgiven, and that forgiveness would lead to his healing. Then James tells us to "confess our sins to one another, and pray for one another, that (we) may be healed."

In their book *Happiness Is a Choice*, Drs. Frank Minirth and Paul Meier make a startling statement. In discussing the causes of depression, they explain that pent-up anger has been the root cause of so many physical illnesses. Science has discovered that people who are depressed have a decreased amount of a chemical called norepinephrine. Norepinephrine is a neurotransmitter that floats in the synapsis between two nerve cells in the brain. Apparently, we need this. What's truly amazing to me is to see what happens to our physical bodies when we have pent-up anger. Since I'm not a doctor, I'll allow the Minirth/Meier boys to take over. The following quote is pretty technical, but I think you'll get the point.

"It has been found that in cases of depression there is an elevation of cortisol (stress hormone) levels in the blood. When cortisol levels are increased, lymphocytes (certain white blood cells) are suppressed. Lymphocytes produce antibodies. With *fewer antibodies*, the individual becomes more susceptible to nearly all physical illnesses.

In other words, pent-up anger results in decreased norepinephrine, which results in increased ACTH (adrenocorticotropic hormone) releasing factor from the hypothalamus, which results in increased ACTH from the pituitary gland, which results in increased cortisol release from the adrenal gland (near the kidneys), which results in decreased lymphocytes, which results in decreased antibodies, which results in susceptibility to nearly all infectious diseases. *Pent-up anger is probably the leading cause of death*" (emphasis theirs).[6]

Wow! In other words, our bodies cannot handle pent-up anger. It's no wonder the Holy Spirit had James write down the words in verses 1:19-20. We should be slow to anger because our anger (the Greek word for anger here indicates a slow, deep-seeded, boiling anger) never produces the righteousness of God. God has never intended for anyone to experience the physical illnesses that are caused by pent-up anger. Why? Because God has never intended for us to have pent-up anger. Not only is it bad for our health, but it's bad for our heart, as well. It's called sin.

In Ephesians 4:26, Paul writes the following:

> [26]**"Be angry, and do not sin":** do not let the sun go down on your wrath.

When the sun went down on *my* wrath years ago in a difficult ministry, the wrath began to dig a deep pit in the bottom of my heart. Then it slowly started to churn and sour and spoil. I can recall the smell of the stench of my anger as it had caused my insides to begin their slow, decaying process. I had been emotionally beaten for more than two years in this ministry. I was hurting, and I couldn't seem to find comfort.

The stagnant pool of my bitterness was permeating—seeping through my vessels and poisoning the rest of my body. My early death lingered. Time passed by and my bones were dried up. I began having mild anxiety attacks, and depression started to cave in on me. After a few months, the anxiety attacks worsened. They left me dysfunctional, unproductive, and useless. My wife was scared for me, and my kids wondered what was wrong with me. My depression grew within me like a cancerous cell as it metastasizes.

It was a cycle with me: I would feel like something horrible was happening—like I was walking on thin ice that could break at any time. Sometimes it would even put me on the floor, and I couldn't move. Every muscle in my body was tightened. Then I would be very irritable. This would last for a couple days, and then it would be followed by two or three months of major depression before it finally let up a bit. But it never let up all the way. I stayed depressed for about two years.

I finally went to see my doctor who prescribed medication for my anxiety and depression. While this helped eliminate the symptoms, I gained great counsel and found that it was my pent-up anger that was the root cause of my physical problems. Once I confessed in great detail my sin of pent-up anger to God, to my family, and to a few close friends, I gained much insight and wisdom about myself, about truth, about God's mercy, about forgiveness, and about how to handle anger, and the healing process within me began.

Once I realized and confessed this bitterness, I felt like a ton of bricks was lifted off my chest. I had allowed others in my life to help me carry this burden. The result was that there was freedom in my life. It was so good to know that I had close friends around me who *really* knew me, accepted me as I was, and helped in my recovery from my anger issue. And it was deeply encouraging to know that my wife understood and supported me. Confessing it to her brought her much-needed freedom, too.

Yes, pent-up anger is the same as bitterness. This sin leads many to infectious diseases. This sin is probably the leading cause of death. So James tells us to confess our sins to one another and pray for one another so we can be healed of our sicknesses. Drs. Minirth and Meier explain how to handle our anger: verbalize it.

I am amazed at how many of the Psalms are David's releasing of his anger toward God. I'm convinced that is the reason why David made it through life. David survived the trials of his life because he brought his anger to God. Granted, the passage in James 5:16 doesn't specify a certain sin, but the principle can be translated to any sin. Verbalizing our sin to someone close to us and verbalizing our sin to God does wonders for the physical body, the mind, the emotions, and our souls. It helps us to see the truth about ourselves. It helps us by allowing others to carry our burdens with us. It helps us to gain a better perspective by hearing the wisdom from godly friends. It helps us to know what to confess to God. It frees us to continue walking with God in the beauty of His mercy and grace, instead of wallowing in our guilt and shame. The load is lifted. Joy begins to be restored. David shouted, "Weeping may endure for a night, but joy comes in the morning!"

I don't think James intends for everyone to tell everyone else in his church all his sinful deeds. That would just be inappropriate. But think with me for a moment. Hypothetically, what would your church look like if everyone was close enough and loved one another enough to unload the burdens that sin has brought? I would venture to say that your church would blossom. I'm convinced that every man should have at least one other godly man in his life to whom he can unload the heaviness of his sin.

Paul told the Galatians, "Bear one another's burdens, and so fulfill the law of Christ." The context is Paul's instructions on how to handle a brother caught in any sin. He tells the ones who are spiritual to do three things: restore, consider, and bear. They were to restore him gently, to consider themselves (in other words, not to be prideful, but to be careful of their own temptation), and to bear the burdens of one another.

Notice Paul didn't tell them to bear *just* the burdens of the brother who was caught in sin, but to bear *one another's* burdens. Why did he say this? Bearing one another's burdens would help each other to *consider themselves* so they are not tempted. Plus, they would be fulfilling the law of Christ, which is to love one another (John 13:34).

I'm thoroughly convinced this is a key ingredient of authentic fellowship. Confessing to one another is sharing your burden with one another so you don't have to bear it alone. The truth is, you really can't bear it alone. You've already proven that. I can't bear your burden, though, if you don't tell me what your burden is. If your burden is a sin, confess it to me so I can help you and pray with you. If your burden is temptation, tell me so I can bear your burden with you. This is authentic fellowship. It's being a partaker of Christ. It's a *together* thing.

But guys don't talk about our burdens. We're too manly. Actually, we're too cowardly. I have seen what happens to men who choose to be cowards. Their wives have left them. Their children have gone with their wives. They have lost their jobs. And many of them are physically and/or emotionally ill because of the sins they have committed. When they are at the end of their ropes, they cry out, "Oh, how I wish I had told someone about my troubles with temptation long ago! If I did, I wouldn't be in this mess!"

Fellowship is deep, not shallow. It's authentic, not fake. But men are usually too afraid to be authentic—far too fearful to ever confess to each other! Let me ask you a question: What are you more afraid of now—confessing your sin or temptation to another godly man who faces the same struggle, or losing all that you hold dear? I think we all know the answer to that one. I plead with you to prayerfully find someone in whom you can confide. All it takes is that first jump and, believe me, you'll be hooked!

There was so much freedom flying through the air at 120 miles per hour. It was so good to know I had a professional firmly attached to my back. The truth is, the Holy Spirit has your back. He's full of mercy. And He has freedom waiting for you. So go ahead…jump.

SECTION TWO:

STARTING THE JOURNEY

CHAPTER FIVE

DRAWING UP BATTLE PLANS

If you plan on nothing, you'll reach nothing every time. When an army goes off to war with the wrong plans of attack and defense, defeat is inevitable. You've probably heard of great warriors throughout the ages who planned and fought courageous battles: Napoleon, Leonidas, MacArthur, Helmuth von Moltke the Elder.

What? You've never heard of Helmuth von Moltke the Elder? I have to tell you about this guy. If anyone knew that armies who went into battle with the wrong plans of attack and defense would be defeated, it was Moltke.

Moltke was a genius at strategizing for war in the 1800's. After graduating from the Royal Military Academy of Denmark, he entered the Danish army for service but resigned in 1822 to join the Prussians. He grew in rank, and word spread of his famed battle tactics. In 1836, the Ottoman sultan, who was about to go to war with Muhammad Ali of Egypt, invited him to serve as military advisor for his army in Armenia. Moltke worked very hard making extensive reconnaissances and surveys, navigating the Ottoman Empire, traveling several thousand miles in his journey.

However, when it was time for the army to go to war with the Egyptians, the Ottoman general refused to follow the advice of

Moltke. The result was horrific! The Ottoman army was severely beaten, the sultan was killed, and Moltke fled to his home in Berlin.

One may predict that Moltke would quit this career and take up fishing, but his abilities for strategizing amazing battle plans continued to develop as he spent the next few years publishing his works. In 1857, he was made Chief of the Prussian Military Staff. Moltke went right to work making several changes to the strategic and tactical methods of the Prussian army. He changed the armament and the means of communication. He improved the training of staff officers. He changed the method for the mobilization of the army. He even established a formal study of European politics that would aid in the plans for their war campaigns. In other words, Moltke quickly put into place a top notch, well-greased machine of an army.

When the Prussians began to quarrel with Denmark, Moltke was asked to develop a battle plan. Can you guess what happened? You got it—the generals did not adhere to his plans properly, and the Prussians lost the battle with the Danes.

If I were Moltke, I would be greatly tempted to take up golf right about now. One would definitely think that Moltke would have given up on advising and strategizing for war when his plans seemed to continue to be refused. But he didn't, and he was finally raised in position to Chief of the Staff for the allied German forces. His battle plans were finally adopted and executed, and the Danish army, defeated, was forced to agree to the German peace terms.

You see, when an army goes off to war with the wrong plans of attack and defense, defeat is inevitable. Moltke had well-thought-out plans, but some refused to listen and tried to fight the battle with their own methods. And they lost. I'll be honest: This sounds a lot like me. When we men seek to fight our battles with our own methods, defeat is inevitable.

Someone has written great battle plans for us—plans that are proven. However, many times we refuse to listen. We fight our battle with the wrong plans, and then we lose that battle only to return the next day with our same lame plans. And guess what? We lose again. This sounds silly, doesn't it? But it's exactly what we do.

And what are our plans? We enlist the best of the best of the best. Major Will Power leads the advance, while General Isolation stands guard at the post. And Lieutenant Firm Determination brings all the heavy artillery of promises never to fail again. All come to our aid, but no matter how much will power we possess, no matter how determined we may be, no matter how many promises we make, losing just seems to be our lot in life.

Men, this is absurd! I refuse to believe that God placed me on this earth, saved me from sin, and told me to be holy, but gave me no plans of attack and defense with which I can fulfill His desires for me to honor Him and to have joy and satisfaction as I walk with Him. I'm convinced we have been fighting with the wrong battle plans.

I'm confident God knew exactly how Helmuth von Moltke the Elder felt. I am reminded of wisdom's call as written in Proverbs 1:

> **20Wisdom calls aloud outside; she raises her voice in the open squares. 21She cries out in the chief concourses, at the openings of the gates in the city she speaks her words: 22 "How long, you simple ones, will you love simplicity? For scorners delight in their scorning, and fools hate knowledge. 23 Turn at my reproof; surely I will pour out my spirit on you; I will make my words known to you. 24 ...I have called and you refused, I have stretched out my hand, and no one regarded..."**

God's wisdom is stretching out her hand to us, men who desire freedom in our journey of life as believers in Jesus. We desire freedom in our thoughts from the lust that has plagued so many of us. We long for freedom in what our eyes gaze upon—knowing that gazing at these things never satisfies. It always, always leads to destruction. We crave the freedom to be at perfect peace that only comes when our minds are stayed upon the Prince of Peace.

God's wisdom is calling out to us, pleading with us to accept her, embrace her, live by her, to never leave her side. She saves lives. She redeems the lost. She upholds the weak. By her the universe was made, and by her temptation is endured.

It is because of her that joy can be experienced through trials. It is because of wisdom that peace may be found in the midst of pain. But we refuse the wisdom that gets us the freedom for which we long. We refuse that which God possesses, proven plans of attack and defense that can win the victory in our lives.

His wisdom is found in His Word. When we think of authentic fellowship among men, we really ought to ask, "Is there a model for us from which we can learn?" Wisdom tells me to look to the One Who created it. I can think of no better place to look than to Jesus Christ, as He exercised authentic fellowship with His disciples.

The King of Abandoned Glory

There is a Christian band from Canada that's beginning to take home all kinds of awards. And rightly so! One of my favorite songs by Downhere is called *How Many Kings*. The lyrics are beautiful as they portray the heart of God that broke because of His love for people. It broke so much so that He sent his only Son, the King, to come where we are, to be what we are, to die for us. How many Kings would do that? And He did that so we can have beautiful fellowship with Him.

You see, it all started when a King abandoned His glory, stepped down from His throne, and came to this lowly place in a lowly way. The Lord of lords put on humanity, grew up in it, and drew a crowd. He apparently had quite a large following, and from this following the Lord appointed a group of seventy people who believed in Him and had followed Him, and he sent these seventy out to proclaim His gospel.

Then, King Jesus chose twelve men with whom He would spend the next three and a half years teaching, showing, proclaiming, training, and experiencing the most glorious and extravagant intimate fellowship the world has ever seen. These intimate years spent with the Creator God changed these men from their core.

And out of this small group of scallywags and riff-raff whom the King loved, Jesus chose three men to be His inner circle. These three were allowed to see things and experience things the rest of the group wasn't. And out of this inner circle of three was the disciple whom Jesus loved. This was the disciple who wrote about fellowship in 1 John.

Everything mentioned above has me asking questions. I don't know the answer to some, like why did Jesus choose to have a group of seventy? We obviously see what He did with them in Luke Chapter 10, but why seventy? Why not seven hundred or even seven thousand? It seems to me that Jesus could have gotten a lot more headway with His gospel with seven thousand people!

Why did Jesus form an inner circle with Peter, James, and John? What were the commonalities between these guys? We know that they were all once in the fishing business together (Luke 5:20; Mark 1:19). We know that James and John were brothers. The Scriptures seem to elaborate on their flaws more than the others, too. Peter had foot-in-mouth disease, and three times he denied he knew the King. Jesus even called him Satan once!

Jesus had a special name for James and his little brother, John: The Sons of Thunder. Those boys actually wanted to call down fire from heaven and kill a bunch of Samaritans! How's that for a disciple of Christ?[7] Then, they had the audacity to ask Jesus if they could each sit on one side of His throne in heaven. This surely made the other disciples quite jealous, but these are the three He chose as His inner circle.

It seems that Peter, James, and John were full of zeal. I'm sure He enjoyed their zealous personalities; after all, He did create them. Surely their zeal was expressed in many positive ways and not only the negative ones just mentioned. After all, our number one strengths can also be our number one weaknesses. Maybe they needed more work than the others, so Jesus spent more time with them. Perhaps, because of their zealous personalities, Jesus spent more time with them to teach them how to channel all that energy. It does seem that Jesus rebuked these boys quite a bit!

Let's take a look at good ol' Peter. One writer describes his personality as "hopeful, bold, confident, courageous, frank, impulsive, energetic, vigorous, strong, and loving, and faithful to his Master notwithstanding his defection prior to the crucifixion."[8] Indeed, it was Peter who attempted to walk on the waves toward Jesus. It was with regard to Peter's confession of Jesus as the Christ that Jesus said to His disciples, "Upon this rock I will build my church." It was Peter who questioned Jesus while the Master was washing His disciples' feet. It was Peter who grabbed the sword and cut off Malchus' ear. It was Peter to whom Jesus asked if he loved Him. And it was Peter who preached that fearless sermon in Acts Chapter 2. It definitely appears that Peter became the leader of the Apostles shortly after Jesus' ascension. Peter definitely had a zealous, energetic personality.

It is said that James and John were probably the sons of Salome, the sister of Mary, Jesus' mother. So, perhaps Jesus and these two brothers grew up with each other. It would be natural for Jesus to continue to invest in them since there was already a relationship there.

Now, I'm not suggesting that Jesus loved to be around these men because He liked energetic people more than nonenergetic people. I'm convinced that Jesus had a plan. And part of His plan was to use these guys and their personalities to fulfill a major portion of ministry leadership in their near future. Remember, Jesus spent tons of time with all twelve of these men. But these three guys had a special relationship with Jesus for a special purpose.

And why did Jesus seem to be best friends with John? Did He need this for His sake, or for John's sake, or both? We see the one who laid his head on the chest of the King at supper time (Jn. 13:23). We see the one who stood by Jesus' mother when He was dying on the cross (Jn. 19:26-27). This was the one called "the disciple whom Jesus loved." John was sincere and loyal.

And he was a son of thunder. He was the only one who was courageous enough to stand at Mary's side when the other disciples ran and hid. John was a changed man. Sure, the other disciples were changed, too, but John was *really* changed. He was definitely changed by the fellowship he had with Jesus while He was on the earth. Those rebukes John received from Jesus surely sank deep into his heart. I can't imagine what thoughts and feelings ran through this disciple as he stood there and watched the life leave his Master's torn body.

The reason Jesus came was to save that which was lost. His mission was to establish His body on earth called the Church, and He used the disciples to do precisely that. I'm sure there are several more reasons why Jesus had these groups, but I'd like to offer one suggestion and expound on it. Perhaps Jesus wanted and needed the fellowship with these men—not to keep Him from sinning, but for the camaraderie. After all, humans are created for it, and Jesus is fully human. He is also fully God, so He delighted divinely in the fellowship He had with them.

It was the inner circle of three to whom Jesus chose to express His glory in the Transfiguration. It was these three men whom Jesus chose to be with Him and pray while He suffered in the garden just before His death. Could it be? Could it really be that the King of kings actually needed comfort from His three closest friends? Could it be that Jesus actually wanted these three to experience the joy of witnessing His glory at the Transfiguration? As future leaders of the Church, they saw the glory of the Christ, and this glory had seared their thoughts about Him as it was permanently engraved in their minds and hearts.

I'm suggesting that Jesus delighted in the special friendship He had with Peter, James, and John. Yes, the King of glory wanted and needed authentic fellowship.

I'm suggesting that Jesus chose the 70 to be part of His glorious work on earth. I'm suggesting that He chose the 12 to be part of His deeper purpose for coming. I'm suggesting He chose the 3 to share in the more intimate times with Him, and He chose the 1, John—who was probably the youngest of the 12—with whom Jesus could show what real, authentic fellowship looks like and feels like on a one-on-one basis.

Can you imagine one-on-one time with Jesus? You will experience it one day if you've trusted in Him alone for your salvation!

Jesus showed John what His fellowship is supposed to be like. He personified love, perfect love, in the form of the bond of friendship that can never be broken, for nothing can separate us from the love of God (Rom. 8:35-39). This love was, and is, all-giving, sacrificial, directed toward people who don't deserve it, and the first to take initiative. Jesus loved John with the love that He created, and it changed John's life forever.

In fact, John's life was so changed by the love of Jesus that he was willing to suffer physical torture and permanent abandonment for spreading that love. And did he ever experience physical torture! Traditional Christian history tells us that he was boiled alive in hot oil and survived. And he was sent to the Isle of Patmos in exile for the rest of his life. The intimate fellowship he had with Jesus changed him into the man he became. It's no wonder that John was the one who wrote about the love of God and His fellowship. He experienced it the most. He experienced it to the fullest, and it brought him ultimate joy.

The Battle Plan: Your 70-12-3-1

Yes, I think it could be that Jesus wanted and needed fellowship with these men. Our heavenly Father delights in the fellowship we have with Him now. Jesus wanted that fellowship because He is divine. He needed that fellowship because He is human.

This means a lot to me. Jesus *wants* my fellowship. He wants YOUR fellowship! He wants us to be His partakers—His metochoi. He calls us to be so. And He tells us in order to be His metochoi—to be His close friends—we must be deeply involved with other believers, enjoying the exhortation with one another. I believe He showed us how to accomplish the fellowship we need with one another. Perhaps we need *our* 70-12-3-1.

Now, I'm not saying we should go out and find exactly seventy people, twelve men, and draw three from them. And I'm definitely not proposing that we should play Jesus by doing exactly what He did with these groups of people. I'm only suggesting that we use, as a basis, how Jesus chose to experience fellowship with His disciples as a model that we can apply to our lives. I'm suggesting that these numbers, 70-12-3-1, could be representations of groups of people with whom you can experience authentic fellowship, just as Jesus did. I think it would be wise to model our relationships with other people the way the Wonderful Counselor did His. Here's how this could work.

Your 70

First of all, the 70 should represent your local church. Since Jesus came to set up His body on the earth called the Church, and the apostles planted local churches, then perhaps we should utilize our local churches for fellowship. (That's a novel idea!) The author of Hebrews tells us not to forsake the gathering of the assembly (10:25), and we just got finished looking at what biblical fellowship is. The purpose of these local churches (metaphorically, our 70) includes worship, teaching of the Word, fellowship, prayer, edification, evangelism, and service. Every Christian man should be involved in some way with his local church, utilizing his God-given spiritual gifts.

Let me make something clear: The local church isn't something we attend; it's something we are. Remember, ministry is people. It's not a place, or a building, or a set of programs. It's people like you and me. Flawed people. Stupid people. But precious people nonetheless. People who need the comfort and conviction that comes from hearing God's Word preached and from fellowshipping with God's people. But if you're not authentic, you will not relate to people. You'll have a failure to connect.

You really do need your 70. And your 70 need you. Forsaking them hurts both you and them. What's worse is that the Church cannot fulfill our purpose of spreading the glory of God to the world unless we are truly loving God and loving one another.

But I'm convinced we need more than just our 70.

Your 12

Your 70 supplies your 12. Again, it doesn't have to be exactly twelve people, and I don't think it necessarily has to be men only. You may already have your 12. Your 12 could be your Sunday school class or small group (if your church has small group ministries). It could be a group of married couples who are authentic and encouraging to one another regarding their marriages. It could be a group that you start on your own, but I'm suggesting that it's drawn out of your 70, i.e., your local church. Whatever group it is, I propose that this needs to be a group where there is less Bible study and more emphasis on fellowship and prayer. Before you scourge me for stating that, let me clarify.

Everything has to have a purpose, and local churches must have a balanced set of goals that fulfill their purpose for existing. The purpose of a local church, as stated before, includes worship, teaching of the Word, fellowship, prayer, edification, evangelism, and service. Many churches are heavy in one area and light in another. While understanding that every church is unique in its needs, I'm suggesting that your 12 takes what is taught from the Scriptures on Sunday mornings and seeks to apply it specifically to their lives as couples or individuals. Because this is a smaller group, your 12 should be the perfect place for more authenticity to occur. (Bear in mind it can be more difficult and even inappropriate to be too open if this is a mixed group of men and women.)

Your 12 should provide the atmosphere for real talk, for deeper fellowship, for someone to share real struggles, for confession, healing, forgiveness and reconciliation. There should be the sharing of laughter together, joy and excitement together. It should be a place where you can share your pain and suffering, knowing that you have a few others who understand and won't abandon you. Your 12 should very well be what you need to become free from whatever has you bound. This should be your place to share things that you couldn't share with your 70.

You may want to say at this point, "Chad, there is no such place like this within my 70. What do I do now?" While I can't be your Holy Spirit (and believe me, you don't want me to be), I can suggest that you share this book with your pastor and tell him that someone needs to champion this ministry in your church. Keep in mind, however, that your pastor may very well be looking that champion in the eyes as you speak to him. You could be the catalyst that turns your Sunday school class or small group into something far more genuine than it has ever been—taking the Scriptures that have been taught and bringing them to life in each of you. You could be that champion that starts a group of 10 or 15 guys who meet weekly for authentic fellowship. Having the approval of your church's spiritual leadership, you could be the influencer that changes the men in your church from bystanders to real leaders. It could start with you.

I pastored Faith Bible Church in La Marque, TX for 2 ½ years. We had a small group that met on Wednesday nights. The church was made up of about 50 people, so our Wednesday prayer meeting was a small group of people—around 15. This group, made up of men and women, had really bonded well over time. While I was there, we instituted the little game called the Honor Chair.

These folks really love the Honor Chair game. Here's how it works: We all sit in our chairs in a circle, and I choose one person to be on the Honor Chair. This person doesn't actually have to move to another chair; they can stay where they are since we are in a circle. Every person must say something uplifting to the one on the Honor Chair. What they say cannot have anything to do with their outward appearance. In other words, one shouldn't uplift him by saying that he has cool tennis shoes. They must say something uplifting about his character, something special he has done, his personality, how he loves his wife and kids, his use of his spiritual gifts, etc. And everyone must say these things directly to him, rather than to me, the leader (which, for some reason, is not so easy to do).

So we go around the circle and, one by one, each person speaks encouraging words to the one sitting in the Honor Chair. While at Faith Bible, we must have played that little game at least a dozen times, and every time there wasn't a dry eye in the room by the time we were finished. Even the macho men were touched emotionally by the words of affirmation and encouragement. I have noticed two things as my church has conducted this activity: 1) It's uncommon for everyone to speak uplifting words to another, and 2) it's not easy for everyone to receive uplifting words from others. We have to learn how to really uplift someone, and we have to learn how to receive those blessings with gratitude.

As we continued to conduct the Honor Chair, another principle was learned by all of us. We eventually began to become a bit more authentic with each other. As we sought to take to heart what I preached the previous Sunday morning, the people in this small group began to share real struggles and real heartaches. And something great started taking place. Just like we did in the Honor Chair, when someone opened up and shared a struggle, the rest began to speak words of affirmation, empathy, and encouragement directly to them. In the past when someone tried to open up, everyone else just remained silent and still. Those reactions can really kill authentic fellowship! But our group has learned that authenticity among one another is liberating.

There can be quite a ministry in your 12. I'm willing to bet that your 12 would love that kind of ministry, too.

Your 3

Most men may already have their 70, and a few may have their 12, but even fewer have their 3. I have asked several Christian men who attend church each week three questions. The first question I asked was if they have *within their church* any number of men with whom they experience this type of complete authentic fellowship we have been discussing in this book. I'm talking about an inner circle of men with whom they can share all their secrets and know they will not receive condemnation but rather loving encouragement to confess and keep on keeping on. It's an inner circle of brotherhood where their closest friends can pray for *deeper* needs. It's a place where a man can feel free to share things he might not be able to share with his 12. Your 3 is a small group of men with whom you would want to spend more time. It's your rest haven—your home away from home. Burdens are shared and carried by each other.

You need your 3. Your 3 know more about you than your 12. They humble you by confronting you in love and uplift you through gentle exhortation. You find that you can persevere better knowing that your 3 not only know all about your struggles but will ask you how you're *really* doing. They can most likely tell if you're lying, but the truth of the matter is that you probably won't lie to them because *you're* the one that would end up being hurt by lying to those in your inner circle. When I asked several men if they had this type of relationship within their churches, the vast majority of them answered with a resounding "NO!" But they all wish they did.

The second question I asked them is how their wives would feel if they knew their husbands were involved in a small group of men where authentic fellowship took place. All of them (who were married, of course) said their wives would feel much more secure if they knew their husbands were involved with this type of men's group. The third question I asked these men is if they feel it's okay that the men in their churches are not experiencing this authentic fellowship. Their answer, once again, was an emphatic "NO." The men I interviewed all long for this kind of fellowship.

So how does one start his 3? Here's the answer: His love must overcome his fear (1 Jn. 4:18). Remember what love is? It's all-giving, sacrificial, directed toward those who don't deserve it (which is every man), and it takes *first initiative*. This love must overcome fear, and this is only done by the Holy Spirit Who lives inside you. You may have fear that if you ask three or four guys at your church with whom you sense a good connection, they'll laugh at you and think you're a little too feminine because you want to talk about your feelings! Or you're afraid they might think you're some kind of pervert. The truth is, they really need an inner circle of three, four, or five. However, because you are drawing your 3 out of your 12, you should know them well enough to realize they'll jump on the opportunity you propose. Submitting to the Spirit, Who gives strength and fills with love, you can obtain your 3.

Take first initiative by prayerfully choosing your 3 out of your 12. Invite them to your favorite restaurant or coffee shop and lay out your ideas on the table. Explain the purpose. There is some great resources available to you, such as Samson Society (www.samsonsociety.net) or Men's Fraternity (www.mensfraternity.com).

All Christian men need their 3. Even the Savior needed His 3. If the men in your 12 were honest with themselves, they would admit their desire to have their 3, as well.

Your 1

Men, this is the most important. This is most important for the whole Church. In fact, I'm convinced having a 1 is foundational. Let me explain why. It seems that Jesus had a best friend. Out of this relationship, John was personally mentored by the King of kings. There was quite a unique and powerful fellowship that solidified John's faith, theology, and worship. This one-on-one authenticity tore him, purified him, and then built him. It changed him at his core. It caused magnificent differences in John mentally, spiritually, emotionally, and even physically. How a guy can withstand to be boiled alive in oil and still have the nerve to spread this love of Jesus is way beyond me. But he did. The friendship Jesus and John shared must have been spectacular! Best friends with Jesus—surely there has never been a more trusting, intimate fellowship between two people since these two. Yet I believe we are called to pursue this.

I believe every man needs a 1. Your 1 may come from your 3, or he may come first. But every man needs a 1 to challenge, pour his life into, mentor. And this 1 can do the same with him.

It's more than just a friend, far more than an acquaintance. But get this—the thing about this 1 is that he probably will be a lot different from the best friend you had back in high school or college. And if you are in high school or college now, you might need to rethink who your 1 is or might be. In fact, whatever your age may be, when you start to work through your 70, 12, and 3, you might very well find that you need to change who your 1 currently is, or change the way you think your 1 should or could be. You might even need to change who your 3 should be as well. Proverbs 13:20 says it best: "He who walks with wise men will be wise, but the companion of fools will be destroyed" (NKJV).

Yes, you may find that your 3 isn't the kind of inner circle that is lifting you up and helping you walk in the Light. You may need to find a new 3. But I wish to go a little further regarding the 1, for many of you already have your 1 and actually had that person even before you had your 70, 12, 3. Those of you to whom I am referring now should *never* change your 1 because you are spiritually and legally bonded to that person.

This book is mainly written to change the way churches do men's ministries. But some books on men's ministries tend to focus so much on men and their needs that they leave out the foundational relationship. Some books that propose so much accountability and camaraderie among men tend to leave out the holiest and most sacred human-to-human relationship ever created. Before Christ set up His Church, before God called Abraham to be the father of the nation of Israel, even before the existence of civilization, God made husband and wife.

This holy matrimony is the foundation of all other institutions. All throughout history countries fell when the family disintegrated. Men, I strongly and emphatically propose that no Christian, married man will sufficiently benefit from authentic fellowship among other believers if he is not experiencing authentic fellowship with his wife. If you are more authentic with your 3 than you are with your wife, you have flipped God's design for freedom upside-down. Freedom begins in the home. Freedom starts in the relationship you have with your bride.

My wife and I seek to emphasize this in our marriage. I am working hard at becoming more and more open and transparent with Melissa. We talk to each other about our personal struggles. As we grow closer together, we are learning each other better.

We are learning where our deepest struggles lie, and we are growing more and more compassionate toward each another. Sometimes it hurts her to hear what my deep struggles are, but this has built a tremendous trust from her toward me. She knows that I wish to keep no secret from her. I want her to see and know the real me—all of me. Guess what? She really wants to know the real me, too. She doesn't necessarily need to know the day-to-day battles, but she does need to know that I have battles, and what they are.

Some guys think that their wives wouldn't be able to handle hearing of their struggles, and I used to think that, as well. Some guys think that it would be better just to tell their 3 about their addiction to Internet porn or whatever their struggle is. I disagree. I'm convinced that this authenticity that I've been dealing with in this book begins with the most sacred relationship on earth. Don't talk about your struggles with your 3, or anyone else, unless your wife knows about it first. And if you are afraid of what she may do... good. You should be. That's the way it's supposed to be. Welcome to the Journey to Freedom.

But you're not alone on the journey; you have the Holy Spirit to guide you and to comfort you and your wife. And you have your 3 to support you and your wife with prayer and shoulders. If you think of yourself as a manly man, you may be surprised to find that you need your friend's shoulder. And you'll definitely need the prayer. And you have your 12 and 70 to provide encouragement and healing. (They should provide this if they practice authentic fellowship.) This is the way God intends His Church to be—a safe place for people to journey to freedom together.

You see, guys, our wives are not just our lovers. Scripture says you and your wife are one in the flesh. God created marriage so that the husband and wife can be naked together and not be ashamed. Talk about freedom!

But she's also your friend. She's supposed to be your best friend. Be naked with her physically. It's biblical, and it's fun! But also be naked with her emotionally, spiritually, and mentally. That's also biblical, and it most definitely leads to freedom. I love having nothing to hide. There's no weight, no burden holding me down.

Now many of you are probably saying about now, "That's great, Chad, but I'm not married." My answer is, "That's great, Reader. Neither was Jesus." That's why He had John. It would be unwise for a man to choose a woman as his 1 unless he was married to her. The kind of fellowship mentioned in this book is so transparent and intimate that a great bonding would take place in a one-on-one relationship. Therefore, if you are single, I suggest you choose a solid, Christian man from your 3 with whom you can share this authentic fellowship. This is what Jesus did. But if at some point you stand at the altar and say, "I do," your bride must take the place as your 1.

The Progression of Authentic Fellowship

Since marriage is the foundational relationship for any institution on earth, including the Church, then everything that is good for an institution flows from the marriage. In other words, our institution, the Church—your 70—benefits from good marriages in it. The strength of any institution, whether it is a Mom and Pop business, the local church, or even a nation, is in direct proportion to the strength of the family units within that institution. And such goodness, such as authentic fellowship, flows from this foundational relationship. It makes so much sense. Ministry is people. People are made for relationships. Remove the foundational relationship, and you remove ministry. In fact, a whole nation would ultimately be removed.

So then, I see a progression of authentic fellowship that springs from the family unit within each local church. To change a local church from shallow acquaintances to having authentic fellowship, one must start at the foundation—the marriage. If there is authentic fellowship taking place between the husband and his wife, then there will be authentic fellowship between the husband and his 3 close friends. If he is lying to his wife, he is more than likely going to lie to his 3. Being real and honest and transparent with your wife is detrimental to the health of your 3.

After time has passed and God's Spirit has been evident among your 3, then there will be real and honest and transparent fellowship among your 12. After time has passed with this authenticity leading your 12 to freedom in Christ, then there will be real and honest and transparent fellowship among your whole church. But it all starts at the foundation—your 1.

I hope you are seeing the bigger picture here. If you are married, the quality of your relationship to your wife is detrimental to the health of your local church, and thus to the Kingdom of God! It is no wonder that churches are failing in authentic fellowship. It is no wonder that nations are collapsing. Families are falling apart. The time is now for Christian men to decide to become real men—authentic men.

So the progression is simple. Fellowship begins with friendship. Whether you are married or single, friendships are built as you begin with your 70, and fellowship deepens as you begin with your 1.

The Time Factor

I was with a group of men one time who wanted to be committed to each other in friendship and accountability. I was helping them learn how to be authentic with each other so they could help each other in their walks with the Lord. We hadn't been together very long in this new ministry and were really just continuing to get to know each other better, but one guy didn't seem to take that into account.

We were making small talk, and out of the blue this guy blurts out, "Well, let's report to each other! I haven't masturbated at all this whole week. Okay, how about you guys?" As you can probably guess, there was a hush that fell on the group.

Some guys are just more open than others. With most guys, however, it takes time to build authenticity. If I don't know you, I don't want you to know too much about me. The reason is simple and logical. I don't know what you will do with the information you would have about me. And this information is critical to my reputation with other people. Are you a gossiper? Are you judgmental and critical of others? Do you get thrills out of hearing other guys' struggles? Are you really here to help carry burdens, or do you just want to see the baggage of other people? I realize that not all men are like this. Some are more trusting than others. But not every man is like that, and one must take that into account in order to rightly pursue authentic fellowship with him—especially when a man has been betrayed before.

Sometimes people remove their masks too soon. And when they do, it aggravates and irritates something that's already there—fear. That's why the 70-12-3-1 principle works. Because *it takes time* to work through it. It isn't the *end*, but it is the *means to the end*. It is the context for God to work. It works through something that God has already established and in which He already works—the Church.

It is a method of fellowship for the Holy Spirit to accomplish His perfect plan in the lives of believers.

I'm convinced too many Christian men are fighting their battles with the wrong battle plans. The truth is our God, our Supreme Commander-in-Chief, has orchestrated a magnificent masterpiece of a battle plan for self-defense and attack. This plan is hidden deep within the fortress called the Church. When we gather there and become deeply involved, we will find that those plans are the people of God, themselves. Men, we desperately need each other. And as the plans mentioned in this book are not the only plans that could work, I know that they do work. I have my own 70-12-3-1. And I have shared this with others, and it works for them, too. Quit fighting with the wrong plans and try these instead. There's freedom waiting for you on the other side.

CHAPTER SIX

THE SHADOW AND THE CHAMPION

God loves your church!

Do you realize that? Do you *really* realize that? He loves, really deeply loves, your local church. Throughout this book, I have attempted to state the biblical mandate of authentic fellowship within the local church. I'm convinced that men isolate themselves, not allowing others to enter their world and not entering others' worlds. Thus, we can't bear one another's burdens. So we all seem to be on a journey to freedom, but most Christian men are driving in their own lanes. And many guys are pursuing their journey to freedom in the same manner the world teaches them to—try harder, man up, pull yourself up by your bootstraps. But, as we all know too well, this simply does not work.

So how does a man enter into the relational involvement with other guys in his church? How do you get new guys in your church to be involved in authentic fellowship? How does a church motivate men on the fringe to take that first step through the 70-12-3-1 process? Perhaps the answer to these questions is found only when we first answer this question: Why do men keep their secrets?

I'm convinced the major reason why Christian men in churches keep their secrets, as mentioned in Chapter 4, is because we have fear. We are afraid. I already wrote a little bit about how to overcome that fear—through love. Jesus loves the Father and thus obeys Him. Jesus obeyed the Father by being the perfect sacrifice for our sins because Jesus is also passionate for people. Jesus humbled Himself, and the Father made Him the Champion by exalting His name above all other names.

We should love the Father and obey Him. We should obey the Father by loving people. Through our love for God and passion for people, we should sacrifice our fear and champion the cause of authentic fellowship in our churches.

The purpose of this book is to free up the Church to take the ideas written here and run with them. Make them happen. Put them into play. But someone has to decide to run. I am challenging you to be that someone. I am challenging you to sacrifice your fear on the altar of Christ's love and run with these ideas. I am challenging you to champion the cause of authentic fellowship in your church.

The Shadow

"Who knows what evil lurks in the hearts of men? The Shadow knows...Heh-heh-heh-heh-heh-heh-heh...!" Okay, okay. I'll explain. If you're an old guy, you know from where that quote came. (It was my father-in-law who introduced me to The Shadow.) But for the rest of us young'uns, allow me to fill you in.

Back in the 1930's, families would sit around their radios and listen to the Detective Story Hour. There was this main character called The Shadow, a fictional vigilante and one of the most famous pulp heroes of the 20th century. Apparently, he was a pretty cool hero because he had "the power to cloud men's minds so they cannot see him." The Shadow would cast fear into the hearts of his victims or anyone who came across his path. This fear inside his opponents would lead to his victory every time. He was the crime-fightin' Master of Darkness. No one could defeat...The Shadow (insert eerie theme music here).

Now allow me to tell you why I brought up this old school vigilante in a book about authentic fellowship among men. Some time ago, I asked a group of men this question, "What keeps men from being REALLY honest with one another?" The responses were fantastic.

Scott gave me permission to share his response with you: "For me, fear and cynicism. Fear that I'll be rejected for exposing my weaknesses and cynical in thinking that others are too busy fig-leafing their own lives to care about mine. However, I am discovering that 1) fear is a shadow best dealt with by pressing through to the light on the other side, and 2) the more I affirm my humanity by being transparent and honest, the more I free you to do the same with me."

Wow. What a statement! Fear is a shadow; it's not a brick wall. It, in itself, has no power to stop us. "For God has not given us a spirit of fear, but of power and love and of a sound mind" (2 Tim. 1:7). This fear mentioned here in 2 Timothy is a *cowardly* fear. As I said before, the reason why we men are not authentic with each other in our fellowship is because we are cowards.

This cowardly fear is NOT of God. Cowardly fear has "the power to cloud men's minds so they cannot see" God. Fear has the power to cloud men's minds and prevent them from enjoying the authentic fellowship that Jesus wants so much for us to have. But fear only has that power if we allow it. Why? Because fear is only a shadow. And with this kind of shadow, guys, we have the power to press "through to the light on the other side." Thanks, Scott. I couldn't agree with you more.

Scott also said, "...the more I affirm my humanity by being transparent and honest, the more I free you to do the same with me." This is what I mean by becoming a champion of authentic fellowship in your church. When you champion the cause, others will follow.

The Champion

Everyone has fear from time to time. Even the Apostle Paul had fear. You don't believe me? Take a good look at Acts 4:

> [29]**Now, Lord, look on their threats, and grant to Your servants that with all boldness they may speak Your word...** [31]**And when they had prayed,**

the place where they were assembled together was shaken; and they were all filled with the Holy Spirit, and they spoke the word of God with boldness.

Do you see that? Paul needed God to help him overcome his fear and be bold. That's what made Paul a champion. He wasn't fear*less*, he just *overcame* his fear. Champions do that. That's why they are victorious.

You see, guys, Paul was a champion. So is Scott. Now Scott, like the Apostle Paul, probably wouldn't tell you that he is a champion, but I think he is. He would tell you that he is far from perfect. But a champion isn't perfect. He might tell you that he has had failures in his life. But that's what makes a man a champion: realizing and learning from his failures.

He probably would also tell you that he has a long way to go in his journey to freedom, although he is enjoying the freedom he is experiencing so far. But that's just the thing about champions. They understand that they haven't reached *it* yet.

This reminds me of another passage written by Paul. He was writing about how much he wants to know Christ fully, to know His power fully, and to know the fellowship of His sufferings fully. Then he adds something that proves even more that he is a champion. Here, again, is Paul in Philippians 3:

[12]Not that I have already attained, or am already perfected; but I press on, that I may lay hold of that for which Christ Jesus has also laid hold of me. [13]Brethren, I do not count myself to have apprehended, but one thing I do, forgetting those things which are behind and reaching forward to those things which are ahead, [14] I press toward the goal for the prize of the upward call of God in Christ Jesus.

This sounds like a champion to me. You see, men like Scott and Paul realize one thing: Fear is normal, but it can be overcome.

It takes a champion to overcome it. So champions are those who overcome their fears and press onward. You may be wondering why I am dedicating so much paper to the topic of fear, and I'll tell you why. Of all the Christian, church-goin', Bible-totin' men I have talked with regarding their lack of authentic fellowship with other men and their earnest desire for it, they all say the same thing: The reason why they don't have this authenticity they desire so much of is because of fear.

Just read what John, another friend of mine, said about why men keep their secrets: "The fear of man is a killer of true accountability. I hate to say this as a pastor, but the church is not a safe place to be honest and open whether you are a man or woman. Until the church is ready to become an authentic place for those who are struggling on the journey of life, moving down the pathway of sanctification, men and women will keep their secrets!"

Fear, which is only a shadow, is a killer. But when you overcome your fear of rejection, fear of not being accepted by people, fear of what others might think of you, and step out and champion this cause of biblical, authentic fellowship, there will be others who follow. And the ones who follow are the ones who have been eager for something like this for a long time. I'm convinced every man really longs for authentic fellowship deep within his heart. He's waiting for someone to open the door of the cage he's been trapped in and let him out.

You should be the champion. Why not? Why not you? I suggest you take this book to your pastor and other church leaders and propose your idea of starting the 70-12-3-1 process. You probably already have the first two down. You have a church, and most likely a Sunday school class or small group. If you don't, find one. Then, begin prayerfully selecting a group of three to five guys with whom you can open up an authentic dialogue. Be real. Bring up the obvious with these guys with whom you should already have a friendship, and seek to deal with your struggles together.

Spread the word. I'm not suggesting that this process become another program in your church, but I am offering the challenge of men seeking to be real men. Do what works. Start a group. Pray for that group. Just be real. Be genuine. Be authentic.

Champions Persevere

I must take this opportunity to make a statement. Bringing about any kind of change in a church, especially among men, is not easy. Usually these work best when they are started small. And bringing about a change from a shallow fellowship to one that is deep and authentic can be quite difficult. So I want to encourage you to do one thing: persevere.

Have you seen the movie *The Patriot*? Mel Gibson starred in this epic film about the struggle of war to establish this country called America. One of my all-time favorite scenes from any movie is in *The Patriot*.

The American militia had begun to retreat because the Redcoats were marching through. Yet Benjamin Martin (Mel Gibson), who had already lost two of his own sons because of the war, fights his way to the center of the frontlines, picks up the old, beat-up American flag that had been dropped to the ground, and waves it as he desperately yells out an inspirational call for his troops to push forward. His troops knew of his passion for victory; they had seen it firsthand. Now they saw his fierce determination not to give up.

The motivation he gave them on the battle field that day brought about a much-needed change in this land that is still enjoyed today. That change is Freedom. It was an incredible scene of perseverance despite the circumstance, and it worked. America was saved! And even to this day, patriotism is regarded in high esteem to those who possess it.

There is a much-needed change in our churches today. That change is Freedom—freedom from the chains of sexual sin that binds so many men. And this change, which is brought about by a champion, comes with perseverance.

Perseverance is a quality that comes from a close walk with God. As you begin to champion authentic fellowship in your church, realize that Satan is going to hurl all kinds of gunfire your way. There is a battle for the men of your church, and you could be the one who raises the flag and motivates the troops to push forward. You could be the one to bring about a much-needed change among the Christian men in your church. You could bring them to freedom. But you can't give up. You'll need to persevere.

You're probably thinking, "Now wait, Chad. Just what is it that I will have to endure?" That's a great question. One area of difficulty in being authentic with people is that people tend to hurt other people. I'm not suggesting that one should expect a battle with people, but I do know that Satan will work extra hard to thwart our battle plans.

I'll just be honest. Being authentic with people could open up the opportunity for someone to hurt you. Someone *could* judge you. Someone *might* break a confidence. Someone *might* avoid you. But God *is* faithful! And He knows what hurt feels like. When we place our trust in Him to do the things He has called us to do, He gives the peace and grace and strength we need to persevere.

Notice that I didn't say that we place our trust in people. We place our trust in God. Even though we can have trusting relationships with people, even though we can share our burdens with people, we are only to trust God. Let me explain what I mean.

When I put my trust in a person to satisfy my need of acceptance, I'm setting myself up for quite a bit of pain. However, God accepts me just as I am. When I put my trust in a person to help me feel significant, the likelihood is that at some point this person will let me down. Yet God always views me as significant.

There is an obvious difference between trusting in people and trusting in God. The difference is that if a person hurts me, yet my trust for acceptance and significance rests in God, then I realize that God has allowed this hurt to take place. Since He accepts me and loves me just as I am, warts and all, and it is He who is working a good work in me, then I can trust that He is allowing this to perfect me.

So if I were to share a burden with a friend, hoping that he will carry this weight with me, yet he breaks confidence and spreads my burden to other people, I will be hurt. However, my feeling accepted and significant can remain the same because I'm trusting in God to fill those needs—not my friend. God uses my friend to carry the weight, but it is God who fills the need. God uses my friend to show His compassion, but it is God's job to work in my heart. So I look for God to do that heart-work, not my friend.

It's a true statement: People hurt people, even in the Church. After several years in one particular ministry, I became quite beat up and exhausted from the turmoil of hurt people saying and doing hurtful things. I was striving to create authenticity in a dangerous place.

One day, I drove to a harbor near where I live. This harbor had been nearly destroyed by Hurricane Ike just a few months before. Near where I parked my truck, I noticed a house on the edge of the high bank of the bay. The house was in shambles. I felt a lot like that house. Hurting people said and did hurtful things to me for so long. I was done for—angry and depressed. But I had been spending much time with good people and with God. I had spent much time in His Word. I was tired of the ministry, but I knew that God wasn't tired of me.

So that day, seeing that torn apart house, I wrote in my prayer journal the following:

"I see the house after the storm. I see what the waves have done—the damage. It is obvious that wave after wave was beating upon it, tearing off piece by piece, until it became a useless, empty place—good for nothing. Its ruins speak to me loudly. "I AM YOU," it says. It sits lonely, uninhabited, and rotting. And yet the waves still threaten just below the seawall. One can't help but wonder, "When will this happen again?"

O Lord, the waves have pounded me unmercifully. There is nothing left in me. I am useless, torn apart piece by piece. Only You can save me. Only You can restore me. Please hold back the waves. Or make me capable of withstanding them.

Set me high upon a rock where the storm's angry waves can't harm me. YOU are my Rock! My Shelter in the storm. I take refuge in You. Deliver me. Help me. I simply cannot serve You without Your protection and strength. Take this weary heart of mine and pump it full of Your energizing power. But first, mend the broken pieces back together. May Your peace hold me together, for I fear I'll fall apart forever.

I see the house after the storm.

Someone is rebuilding."

There are many men in your church who are hurting. Sure, they might have brought much of their pain upon themselves because of their sin. But they need help. One of my mentors once told me that sheep bite. Another mentor told me that sometimes when a soldier is falling, he might swing his sword. Hurting people say and do hurtful things. And when you, the champion of authentic fellowship, begin to gently lead those hurting people down the journey to freedom along with you, you just might get bitten a time or two. You might get a nick here or there by his swinging sword. When you do, remember the words of Paul, a mentor to Timothy (2 Tim. 1):

> [8]**Therefore do not be ashamed of the testimony of our Lord, nor of me His prisoner, but share with me in the sufferings for the gospel according to the power of God...** [12]**For this reason I also suffer these things; nevertheless I am not ashamed, for I know whom I have believed and am persuaded that He is able to keep what I have committed to Him until that Day.**

Every Christian man must have his 70-12-3-1. It should be a must for every local church. It should be a goal for every family. Sometimes it can be difficult to acquire, but your perseverance will pay off. Dads, husbands, pastors, granddads, sons, young men, and old men should have this. However, it's not all they should have. There's more. For, as you can tell, this is not the end of this book.

CHAPTER SEVEN

CHAMPIONS *PREPARE* FOR BATTLE

When I was in high school, I got this whacked-out idea of joining the school's track team. Joining the track team wasn't the bad idea, but *my* joining the team was. I didn't like to run. In fact, I hated to run. I still hate to run today. But I had friends on the track team, so I decided to give it a try.

On the day of tryouts, I showed up with my tennis shoes laced up, my legs stretched out, and my head held high. I must admit, I looked good. I played the part well. My tennis shoes were new, my shorts were in style, and I sported my school's t-shirt for pride. Then the coach called for a few of us to demonstrate our capabilities. I was so ready.

He told us to line up on the track, so I strutted my stuff onto the rubber track along with the rest of the guys. Coach then instructed us that this was the first part of the try-outs, and we were not to sprint but only jog around the track two times. *This will be such a breeze,* I thought. Wow, was I ever wrong.

Coach yelled, "Go," and we took off. There was an immediate problem. Coach said not to sprint, but it seemed I had no choice. The other guys were clearly jogging, but I had to sprint just to keep up with them! It's not my fault. You see, God gave me short legs.

That's right. That's my story, and I'm sticking to it. After the first time around, my heart was dragging about ten paces behind my rear end.

Somehow, I made it a second time around, and then the coach walked right up to me. He was such a loving kind of guy. After picking me up off the ground, he put his arm around me and began walking me toward the locker rooms. Yes, it was clear I was being escorted. As we walked together, Coach gave me some very important advice. "Son," he said, "I can tell you haven't been running very long. Well, you just can't expect to make the team when you haven't prepared yourself. Start preparing now and maybe next year you'll make the team, okay?"

Those words didn't feel that great that day, but I'm sure glad he said them. He was exactly right. When I got back to the locker room, a friend of mine was tying his tennis shoes, getting ready for his try-outs. He took one look at my red, sweaty face and said, "Oh, no, the coach makes us run two miles for try-outs now?" My reply was low and monotone, "No, I only ran two times around the track." Apparently, I didn't prepare for track tryouts. I just showed up.

Champions prepare for battle. They don't just show up.

For the purpose of writing another book, I have been conducting interviews with a few pastors and church leaders who have undergone the pain of dealing with a church member who has either committed adultery or has expressed his addiction to some sort of sexual sin. One pastor made a comment that is so true. After three years of being a mentor and an accountability partner to the youth pastor who worked with him, the truth came out that the youth pastor had been secretly having an affair with another church member. That pastor, through the pain-stricken countenance on his face, made this correct observation: "Accountability is not the cure-all." And I believe he is correct.

I believe having the 70-12-3-1 is a must for every Christian man, but it's only a means to the end. Don't believe for one second that having your 70-12-3-1 will be the lone antidote to sinful living. The truth is, accountability is not the cure-all for temptation and sin. It's certainly not a guarantee one will stop sinning.

I was an accountability partner with a friend once who had been lying to me for several months. He wasn't unlike many Christian guys in our churches today. He strutted his Christian self quite well. He made his holiness look good. He played the part well. But he was sinking in his ship the entire time. While we can't keep one another from lying, we can do something within our 12-3-1 that could create a greater potential for success at living in freedom.

Perhaps one thing that would help is for us to understand just which tools are essential in preparing ourselves for the battle at hand. I use the acronym PREP. P stands for *prayer,* R is *remove all sources,* E is *equip yourself,* and P means *pick a partner.* I'll elaborate more on this later. But it's not enough that you belong to a Bible-teaching church, or that you are part of a small group, or that you are involved authentic fellowship with a handful of guys, or even that you have one brother in Christ (or your spouse) with whom you have great, intimate fellowship.

These things are beginning steps. We mustn't stop there, but continue in God's plan for freedom to be experienced in our lives. God set up His Church on earth, but He didn't leave us on our own. He is quite involved, or at least He desires to be!

Champions Put on God's Armor

Every successful army goes to battle well-prepared. Every champion knows how to prepare himself. It would be foolish for a soldier to enter into warfare without the proper preparation. He needs to be well-trained. He needs open communication with his commander and with other soldiers. He needs his weapons for fighting and rations for survival, and he needs to understand the tactics of the enemy.

I don't know if you realize it, but the enemy is doing the same thing. He also is well-trained and well-prepared. Yet so many men enter their battles without being prepared. Well-intentioned, church-going men are not well-trained. They may have some communication with their Commander; they may even have great communication with Him. But many have little to no communication with their fellow men—not the real communication that we've been discussing here.

Their weapon, the Word of God, is being phased out of so many churches. And several churches that still have God's Word preached soundly are failing in teaching their men how to apply it properly. In other words, you may know the doctrines of the Bible, but you may not know how those doctrines ought to change your life. And you may have a great support group, but without God's Word, you are powerless.

In Ephesians 6, the Apostle Paul declared the right preparation process a soldier in God's army should have.

> [10] **Finally, my brethren, be strong in the Lord and in the power of His might. [11]Put on the whole armor of God, that you may be able to stand against the wiles of the devil. [12]For we do not wrestle against flesh and blood, but against principalities, against powers, against the rulers of the darkness of this age, against spiritual hosts of wickedness in the heavenly places. [13]Therefore take up the whole armor of God, that you may be able to withstand in the evil day, and having done all, to stand.**

The evil day Paul discusses here is the day of temptation. It could be today or tomorrow. For most of us it's every day. Paul emphatically says to all Christians to be well-prepared before we enter into the battle, when temptation raises its ugly head. But Paul doesn't stop there. He is led by the Holy Spirit to cleverly describe the armor of God in pristine detail.

> [14] **Stand therefore, having girded your waist with truth, having put on the breastplate of righteousness, [15]and having shod your feet with the preparation of the gospel of peace; [16]above all, taking the shield of faith with which you will be able to quench all the fiery darts of the wicked**

one. ¹⁷And take the helmet of salvation, and the sword of the Spirit, which is the word of God.

Using the metaphor of a soldier preparing himself for battle, Paul describes the necessary pieces of armor that a believer in Christ must put on in order to "withstand in the evil day." Putting on this armor doesn't refer to the time when a person trusts Jesus as his Savior, but rather to the many times throughout the believer's life so he can endure temptation. Truth, righteousness, peace, faith, and salvation (deliverance) are the defensive weapons. The word of God is the only offensive weapon. These are the "must-have" pieces of armor for every believer in Jesus.

Here's a scary thought: You can suffer utter defeat with just one of these pieces of armor missing in your life. The soldier's belt was his security, his breastplate guarded his heart, his shoes provided traction, his shield protected him from arrows and swords, his helmet protected his head, and his sword was for offensive and defensive tactics in battle. Would you feel ready for battle if you were missing one of these?

But freedom doesn't come without a cost. There must be battle. No one likes war—we all wish for peace. However, because of the world in which we live, we must fight for our freedom. This is the same for the life of every believer, yet in order for every believer to gain freedom, he mustn't fight alone. What do these pieces of armor look like in our lives? How are they supposed to fit? What are they supposed to do? Read on.

The Belt of Truth

When thinking about your 12-3-1, *truth* is that vital piece of armor that creates security in battle. The soldier hung his weapons and rations on his belt. If he gave up or lost his belt, he would lose all that was attached to it. Talk about security! It was the central place for the tools he needed for survival.

Truth is just that for us. David told God, "You desire truth in the inward parts" (Psalm 51:6). When we are truthful about ourselves, especially the deepest part of ourselves, we begin to build on the security that never fails.

Jesus is the *Truth*. And when we tell ourselves the truth about ourselves, admit to God the truth about ourselves, and tell our 12-3-1 the truth about ourselves, we begin to open up the doors and walk through the corridors of freedom's palace.

This belt also provided freedom of movement for the soldier. There's freedom in truth, but one will always find restriction and binding in falsehood.

Many of God's men lie. Men lie to themselves, deceiving themselves so they believe they really don't have a problem with lust or loving money or neglecting their families. Many men tell themselves they must fight their battles alone. That's also a lie. Many men tell themselves they can never live in freedom from their bondage of sin. That's a lie straight from the pits of Hell. For Jesus, Himself, said it best in John 8.

> **[31] Then Jesus said to those Jews who believed Him, "If you abide in my word, you are My disciples indeed. [32]And you shall know the truth, and the truth shall make you free.**

Remember that word *abide*? It's the word for *fellowship*. Jesus was talking to Jewish believers, saying in order for them to be His followers (or His metochoi, though He was using a different word), they must be engaged in His Word. Only then would they know the truth, for the Word of God is truth. And this truth would set them free. "Free from what?" you ask. That's a great question! The rest of the Jewish people who were there, the ones who didn't believe in Him, asked Jesus that question, too. Then Jesus replied:

> **[34]Most assuredly, I say to you, whoever commits sin is a slave to sin. [35]And a slave does not abide in the house forever, but a son abides forever [36]Therefore, if the Son makes you free, you shall be free indeed.**

Jesus is not a slave in His Father's house. He's the Son. As the Son, He has been given all authority in heaven and on earth (Matt. 28:18). Because He is the Son, He has the power to set free the slave (unbelievers). He whom the Son sets free is *really* free! That doesn't mean we will always live like we are free, but the truth is that we are.

We, as believers in Jesus Christ, have been set free! Sometimes I don't feel free, but the truth is, I am. Sometimes I don't live like I've been set free, but the truth is, I am set free! We are free to experience His love, His joy, His peace. But we are also free to experience the misery of our sin. One leads to the abundant life He has for us to live, while the other leads to destruction. We are free to abide, and when we abide, we don't sin (1 Jn. 3:6). When we don't sin, we have joy. That joy motivates us to continue to abide!

So the belt of truth is our security. When used, it keeps our spiritual pants up so we won't fall. We hang our tools on truth, our weapons and rations on truth. We hang our security on truth. We dwell on truth, and as we do, we can continue toward freedom.

What Does This Look Like?

If you are indulging in sin, you are probably telling yourself lies. "I can overcome this myself," you may say. "I will never get out of this trap," you may say. "I can't tell anyone what I've done. I will not be able to bear the consequences." Those are lies. If you have trusted Jesus alone for your salvation, then there's hope. The truth is that you can't overcome this alone, you can escape the trap of sin, and you can confess your sins to another because God commands it, and He honors those who obey His commands. Freedom is found in truth. Tell yourself the truth about who you really are in Christ. Tell yourself the truth about Who God really is as found in His Word. It may look something like this:

"Heavenly Father, I have screwed up royally. But I know this has not severed the love You have for me. Your mercy and grace, through Your forgiveness, are waiting for me as I confess my sin. Your freedom for me to overcome the power of this sin is available to me. I can be free as I follow in obedience to Your word. Help me to confess my sin to another and begin the process of healing from the brokenness I have brought upon myself. Your power is what will heal me. Your love is what will restore me. Your grace is sufficient for me because You love me."

Truth is foundational. Perhaps this is why Paul listed it first among the armor. The truth is that you can be free. Wrap *that* around your loins.

The Breastplate of Righteousness

The soldier in Paul's metaphor also wore a breastplate that protected his chest. Scripture makes it clear that while sin leads to more sin (James 1:14-15), righteousness leads to more righteousness (Rom. 5:3-4). Lying to your 3 will only lead to more destruction. And falling into temptation despite your 3 will never lead to freedom. However, practicing righteous deeds, i.e., "withstanding in the evil day," gives motivation and joy that will spur one to continue in righteousness.

The reason is because this righteousness, referred to as a breastplate, guards our hearts, which is the seat of our emotions. As sin ruins and wrecks our emotional well-being, righteousness motivates us to live in the wonder of Christ's freedom. For it was for freedom that Christ set us free! And with freedom comes unspeakable joy! This joy is quite motivating.

Putting on the breastplate of righteousness is vital, for even the Lord put this on (Isa. 59:17), albeit not to keep Him from sinning, but because He *is* righteous. James says that when we put this on, the devil will flee (James 4:7). Jesus Christ is called our righteousness in 1 Corinthians 1:30. And when we abide in Him (i.e., fellowship with Him), we are putting into practice what we are: righteous people because of Christ. When we practice righteousness, we are living the reality of what we truly are: righteous people because of the righteousness of Jesus. And His righteousness is in front of our hearts blocking the temptation that the devil sends our way.

Over the years I have received messages from many guys telling me of their newfound freedom. Men are breaking free from habitual masturbation, from viewing Internet pornography, and from visiting sex shops. These men are seeing what it's like to experience the purity in what they think, how they act, what they see, and what they hear.

However, I have never had any man tell me that he is miserable in his purity. None of them ever wish they were back in the darkness. The further they go into practicing righteousness, the further they desire to go. Their righteousness is protecting their hearts because righteous living is freedom-living.

What Does This Look Like?

When Paul tells us to "put on" the armor of God, this means the responsibility is ours. *We* are to put it on and not wait for someone else to come along and do it for us. However, putting on these supernatural pieces of armor does require some help at times. It's much easier to put on righteousness when I'm around others who are putting on righteousness, as well.

Putting on the breastplate of righteousness is just doing right. If you are indulging in sin, you'll need extra help in doing right. You'll need the help of other believers to show you how to stop doing wrong, how to begin doing right, and how to keep doing right. What is interesting about this is that it is only as I am standing on God's truth (the belt of truth) that I have the power to do right (the breastplate of righteousness).

It could look like this: "Because truth sets me free, and the truth is that God's Spirit lives inside me, then I have the power of God, the fellowship of brothers, and the truth of His Word to do right and continue to do right so that I dwell in His freedom. And if I fall, His grace is there to catch me."

The Feet Shod with Peace

It's all about the shoes.

Seriously, in Paul's day soldiers wore special sandals. These sandals had special soles that provided traction so they could stand and fight during battle. If a soldier was fighting with bare feet or with ordinary sandals, he would lose his footing, which could easily cause him to lose his life during the battle.

There is something unique for the believer in Christ. This special defensive addition to the list of armor provides supreme traction for every believer who wears it. It enables the believer to stand firm (just as Paul tells the soldier to stand) during the fiercest battle. Without this piece of armor, the believer can lose his footing and fall to his defeat.

Peace. It's something everyone wants. The peace of God is not the absence of crisis, but something supernatural that only believers can experience during hardship—or battle. What makes a soldier stand firm in the midst of warfare? What causes a man not to fold when the enemy strikes with all his might? It's peace. Certainly all believers must know that becoming a Christian doesn't guarantee automatic peace. And this kind of strength isn't always evident until there's a difficulty that arises. According to God's Word, hardships produce endurance and character (James 1:2-8; Rom. 5:3-4). And these pieces of armor Paul describes in Ephesians 6 are things he tells believers to put on themselves.

Paul says that the soldier's feet are shod (meaning, "bound under") with *preparation* of the gospel of peace. The word *preparation* means to "make ready." In other words, the man of God is to be ready for battle by being firmly grounded. And it is God's perfect peace that enables a believer to stand tall during the roughest of times. By being firmly grounded, standing firm, the man of God will not be moved. Anxiety doesn't blow him over, though he may feel anxious. Fear doesn't force him to his knees, though he may have fear. Anger cannot knock him down, though he has felt anger. These things have no authority over him because he has "the peace of God which surpasses all understanding" (Phil. 4:7). His inner peace is in direct contrast to the raging battle outside. Without this peace of God, the believer will suffer battle inside, as well.

What Does This Look Like?

Paul says in Philippians that in order for us to have God's peace, we must stop thinking certain things and replace those thoughts with better thoughts (Phil. 4:6-8). Feelings always follow our thoughts. When your thoughts are lies you are telling yourself, your feelings will follow suit. If your thoughts are that you can never break free from this trap of sin, your feelings will be that of misery and hopelessness.

But if your thoughts are on truth, then God's peace will become evident in your life, which will enable you to stand your ground when the temptations come. So as you stand on His truth, you are able to do right. Your righteousness will motivate you to keep doing right as your thoughts are continuing on truth. As your thoughts are on truth, His peace will continue to "guard your hearts and minds through Christ Jesus" (Phil. 4:6b).

It can look something like this: "I can stand on His truth because my heart tells me that He hasn't left me, is with me now, and will never leave me no matter what sin I commit. Because I have repented of my sin, His forgiveness is absolute and final. Therefore, I have peace because I think on these things, and I have peace knowing that, with His help, I can endure temptation."

The Shield of Faith

Paul does not say the devil shoots arrows at us. He says the devil shoots *fiery* arrows at us. Perhaps you've seen those movies that depict battle fronts where the soldiers fire off those flaming arrows toward their enemies. Having something to block an arrow is one thing, but having something that is powerful enough to quench fire at the same time is another. The reason the enemy shot those flaming arrows wasn't just so the arrows would look neat as they lit up the night sky. It's because they wanted to catch their opponents on fire, even if the arrows were blocked by their opponents' shields.

Paul talks about a radical shield that is available for every believer in Jesus. This shield will not only protect the man of God from the arrows, but it will also quench the fire from those arrows. Now, that's a cool shield. Some things don't tempt me that much. I can see a nice pair of sunglasses in a store and not be tempted to steal them. But other things crouch at the door and tempt me like crazy. And those temptations sometimes seem to just burn within me until I give in.

For me, it's those times when I really need my 3 or 1. I may pick up the phone and give one of them a call, or see if they are online on my favorite social network so we can chat. I would tell them I'm having "one of those days" where the temptation to lust seems almost overwhelming. My flesh is screaming at me to forget my 3 and go for the sin. My flesh will tell me that they don't have time for me or that I'm a bother to them. My flesh will tell me my sin is much more fun.

If I don't have my shield of faith ready, I'm in trouble. For by my shield—my faith in God's promises, God's character, and God's power—every one of those fiery arrows will be quenched and not harm me. John writes in 1 John 5:4 that it is by our faith that we have victory in overcoming the world.

What Does This Look Like?

Exercising faith in God will destroy the plans of the devil. God tells us to ask for wisdom in faith in James 1. That means that if I ask for wisdom while thinking He probably won't give it to me or He really doesn't care, then James says I am just like a wave of the sea being tossed back and forth between belief and disbelief in the goodness of God. God doesn't reward His children with lack of faith.

He rewards us when we say something like this: "Father, I don't know how You will get me through this difficult situation, but I know You will. I don't know how You can keep forgiving me, but I believe You do. I don't know how You can provide for me, but I trust in Your promises. And what I do know is You never break Your promises, and You never change. You promise mercy and forgiveness when I confess. You promise grace to move on when I repent. You promise power to persevere when I ask for wisdom. I am being tempted to sin, but my faith is in Your promise to provide a way of escape. I stand on this truth."

The Helmet of Salvation

The word *salvation* is sometimes taken by many to mean being saved from Hell each time they see the word used in Scripture. However, the word actually means "delivered." If the context in which the word is used refers to being "saved from one's sin," then *salvation* would mean "saved from Hell." Yet the context in Eph. 6:17 indicates that Paul is telling believers in Jesus to take up this helmet of salvation.[9] Therefore, believers are never to go to battle against the wiles of the devil without having put on their helmets!

While the heart is known as the seat of the emotions, the head is the seat of the mind. If the enemy can get into our mind, he can control our entire body. So Paul instructs the believer to take the helmet of deliverance.

Men, we must, at all costs, protect our minds. For once harmful things get into our minds, our emotions are affected, our bodies are affected, and ultimately our spirits are affected. Have you noticed that you cannot control your emotions? You may think you can, but you can't. In fact, we really aren't told in Scripture to control our emotions. We are told to control our thoughts, though. Take a look at what Paul says in 2 Cor. 10:4-5.

> **4For the weapons of our warfare are not carnal but mighty in God for pulling down strongholds, 5casting down arguments and every high thing that exalts itself against the knowledge of God, bringing every thought into captivity to the obedience of Christ...**

The truth is that our emotions follow our thoughts. So does everything else. If a soldier doesn't protect his head, then one swift blow could end his life quickly. If the man of God doesn't guard his mind, immoral failure could wreck his life. Certainly, we can see that this helmet, indeed, provides the man of God deliverance!

What Does This Look Like?

Many guys have told me that they can't stop thinking lustful thoughts. But according to God's Word, the truth that we must tell ourselves is that we *can* control our thoughts. What is difficult is when I try to control my thoughts by myself. What helps is when I share my thoughts with my 3 because knowing we are on our journey to freedom together gives me support to do right. So when

I have a lustful thought enter my mind, I have faith that God will give me the power to toss it out and replace it with truth.

It may look like this: "That young lady working behind the counter at this grocery store is gorgeous. I can easily undress her in my mind and allow my thoughts to wander from there. However, the truth is those thoughts will lead me away from freedom and into the binding darkness. And I want to be able to tell my 3 that my thoughts this week have been pure. Besides, if I ever acted out these thoughts, the consequences would be pure torture. But nothing in this world, Father, can compare to Your freedom that You have for me! I choose Your joy. For it truly satisfies me forever."

The Sword of the Spirit

So this leaves us with the last in the list, but certainly not the least. The sword of the Spirit is our only offensive weapon as we stand strong during our daily battles. If we are rightly prepared by putting on truth, righteousness, peace, faith, deliverance, and taking up the Word of God, we will certainly be well prepared to live in the freedom that Christ died to give us.

Men, if you don't catch anything else from this book, catch this: How foolish it is for us to ever think that we can live pure lives apart from knowing God's Word! Christ, Himself, battled Satan in the wilderness with the sword of the Spirit. How much more should we battle with this offensive weapon?

Notice, too, that this isn't just any sword. The origin of this sword is unique. Swords are made from metals, and they come in all shapes and sizes, depending on their purpose. No matter the shape and size, though, all swords are limited in what they can do. For example, a soldier can maneuver a shorter sword more quickly than he can a longer one. However, a longer sword might be better for heftier combat. I'm no expert on swords or combat, but it is logical to say there is no perfect sword. They all become dull and are constantly in need of sharpening.

However, the sword Paul speaks of in Ephesians 6 was not made from metal. In fact, it was not made from any material one can find on earth. This sword is supernatural. It was wielded by the Spirit of God, Himself. It was this same Spirit that hovered over the deep waters at the time of creation (Gen. 1:2). It was this same Spirit that came upon Elijah so that he could outrun a king's chariot for over 27 miles (1 Kings 18:45-46). And it was this Spirit, the Spirit of the Living God, who brought forth the Word of God through men of God (2 Pet. 1:21). This sword never needs maintenance. It never gets dull—it is always sharp (Heb. 4:12). I want a sword that this Spirit of God makes!

Men, if we are not living in the Word, we will be losing in the world. All the wisdom from all the books in the world on righteous living do not compare to the sharp wisdom of God's Word that cuts straight to the heart. And, of course, that includes this book. Authentic fellowship with God will never happen apart from His Word. Sadly, many churches have abandoned the Bible. It makes me wonder why so many church-going men are falling in to death traps like pornography.

What Does This Look Like?

Truth is found in the Bible. Get into the Word! Memorize verses about overcoming fear, enduring temptation, and persevering in the Christian walk. You can't fight sin without God's Word hidden in your heart.

What happens, though, is that many Christian men make Bible reading their daily chore instead of their daily pleasure (that is, if they read it daily at all). Have you ever considered reading the Bible for pleasure? Sometimes when reading though the Bible, we get bogged down in the genealogies and all those numbers and then quit. If those parts of Scripture are parts that you don't understand, then read the books of the Bible that you do understand and save those other parts for a time when you can ask someone else their meaning.

I feel it is important to start the day by taking in God's Word— every day, too, not just Sundays and Wednesdays. Sometimes I've reread the same verses each day for several weeks. When I'm battling something, there are some very special passages that really change my thinking about myself and my situation, that remind me of God and His promises, and that show me the need to readjust my mind each morning.

Other times, I'll just read a chapter out of Proverbs or Psalms or both. Still, I may just concentrate on one single verse for that day. In any case, I'm chewing on something holy from God's Word, drawing out the juices that fill my body with His character. That changes me.

So the major point of putting on the armor of God is so we can stand. Otherwise, we fall. Notice to whom Paul is writing in verse 10. He calls them *brethren*. That's a plural word. Perhaps putting on the armor of God is best done in the plurality of likeminded believers. And after he describes those pieces of armor, he tells them to pray. Remember that list of four things from the acronym PREP I listed at the beginning of this chapter? *Prayer* is first in the list. This list is not in addition to what Paul wrote in Ephesians 6. I'm only drawing out four principles that we can apply in our pursuit for authentic fellowship. Let's dig out these four principles.

The PREParation Process

I learned two lessons from my track try-out experience that dreadful day in high school. First, I hate to run. Unless something hideously scary is chasing me, I really hate to run. Second, if I want to be a champion with anything in life, I must prepare myself. This is a true statement if you want to play in any sport, if you want to work in any job, if you want to get married, if you want to raise kids, and especially if you desire to live your life in the freedom that God has for you. We must PREPare! There are four principles I have drawn out of the Ephesians 6 passage. Perhaps you could draw more, but these have worked well for me so far.

- **P**rayer – The journey to freedom is accomplished by relying on God's power.
- **R**emove all sources – The journey to freedom is accomplished by pursuing God's holiness.
- **E**quip yourself – The journey to freedom is accomplished through dependence upon God's resources.

- **P**ick a partner – The journey to freedom is accomplished through trusting God's provision.

PREP. It's an easy way to remember how to prepare ourselves for the battles we face daily. We need to look at each one carefully.

Prayer

Lack of communication disrupts relationships. Whether the relationship is between a husband and wife, employer and employee, senator and state, or man and God, the relationship is disrupted when there is little or no communication. God, however, has made His communication known to us through His Word. What is great is that He has also made it possible for us to communicate with Him.

A pastor friend of mine once told me that prayer is the most powerful weapon for believers and the most neglected weapon by believers. We usually reserve prayer for mealtimes, bedtimes, and Wednesday nights at church or small group. But God says to "pray without ceasing" (1 Thes. 5:17).

Prayer is acknowledging our reliance on God's power. Prayer does change things. Most times, we are the ones prayer changes. It's not God's character that needs changing, but mine. When I surrender and rely on God and His power in me, my difficult situation just might change because of the way I am now responding to it. But even if it doesn't change, I will grow through my difficult situation because I am relying on God's power in me and not my own.

I've got bad news and good news for you. The bad news: I will never, in this life, be free from temptation. Freedom from temptation will come when we are in the presence of the Lord in glory. Now, the good news: I can be free from sin's power. Freedom from sin's power can come today as I rely on God's power within me.

James 5:16 says, "The effective, fervent prayer of a righteous man avails much." The Greek word James uses to describe this kind of prayer is where we get our word *energy*. The energetic prayer of the righteous avails much. The truth is, God loves to hear His people pray. God is moved by the prayers of His people. God moves His people when they pray. Prayer works. It was the very next statement made by Paul in Ephesians 6 after he listed the armor of God. He told us to pray always. Prayer is relying on God's power. The journey to freedom is accomplished by relying on God's power. So how's your prayer life?

By the way, prayer with others is vital. Sure, alone-time prayer is vital, too. Christ spent much time alone in prayer, so I'm not knocking that at all. What I'm saying, though, is that when brothers in Christ pray together, there's a special bonding that takes place. Together, men of God acknowledge their dependence on God, and God likes that. Men ought to pray together. Men's ministries must be bathed in prayer. Your 70-12-3-1 must pray together. But don't limit your prayers just for physical ailments of other people. Pray for your thought-lives, your hidden motives, and for one another as you confess your sins to each other. This is part of the whole reason for having a 70-12-3-1—so you can pray with each other for each other.

All right, let's move on.

Remove All Sources

A few years ago my nephew, Benjamin, kept showing signs of irritability at a very young age. The poor little guy had already had two heart surgeries before age five. Now, his mom and dad needed to find out what was causing Benjamin's behavior to be so erratic. After several tests, the doctors found that he was highly allergic to gluten and that it should be removed from his diet. I was amazed at the difference in my nephew's behavior the next time I saw him. It's hard to imagine that removing this one source could change so much, but keeping gluten out of his diet has made a remarkable change. Little Benjamin is now a happy, bouncing-off-the-walls kid, just like 6-year-old boys are supposed to be.

Some guys try to start their journey to freedom, but they trip over all kinds of rocks, bumps, and potholes. It's not that they are going down the wrong road, but they haven't removed those things that are tripping them up. When they try to remove them by themselves, they usually find out just how heavy those rocks can be. That's when they know it's time to acknowledge they need help.

Several years ago I received a call from a young lady who informed me she found out her husband was getting "way too close to another woman." I gave him a call to see if we could hang out for a while. I spent a lot of time with this brother and soon found out he had an addiction to pornography. The sources of his addiction weren't limited to the Internet. He also had video tapes and magazines hidden around the house. It actually took him a couple of weeks to remember all the places where he stashed his treasury of destruction. But when he did, his addiction to viewing pornographic material began to break.

Another time, I got a call from a young man in his early twenties who wanted to have lunch with me. I traveled into downtown Houston where he was going to college. Starved because I had missed breakfast that morning, I sat down with him to eat. All of a sudden he began to cry. I was slightly taken back; I must admit I looked around the restaurant to see if anyone was watching. I figured he wasn't too happy with the sub sandwich he had ordered.

Well, I quickly found out that wasn't the case. He wept in that restaurant as he confessed his bondage to pornography. As we talked about these temptations that are common to all men and how God always provides a way of escape, I told him about the computer software called Covenant Eyes that I've been on for several years that can keep men and women away from Internet pornography. He got help by purchasing the software that monitors his online activity and made me his partner to receive those reports of that activity via email.

A few weeks later I received some seriously negative reports from Covenant Eyes regarding my friend's online activity, so I gave him a call. We talked for a while (actually, we talk each week now) and he decided to add Covenant Eyes' filter to it. He is now moving much faster on his journey to freedom because he is removing the sources of temptation.

I also suggested that he add his dad as another partner to receive those reports. That means that he needed to tell his dad of his problem. His dad loves Jesus and loves his son, and the discussion went very well. This was another way of removing the source of temptation.

That is exactly what these bumps in the road are that trip men up—sources of temptation. So many guys try to live pure lives, yet they do nothing about the sources of temptation. Living in the South, as many probably know, we combat all kinds of bugs. The worst of all bugs, in everyone's opinion, is the blood-sucking pest called the mosquito. However, down here where I live, they aren't so little. These things are more like giant vampire bats swarming around after each rain!

During the summer months of 2009, we received very little rain. That's both bad and good. It's bad because the land is so dry—in fact, parts of Texas suffered a severe drought. But it's good because the mosquito population became quite minimal! When it does rain, we know that in just two short days those wicked little creatures will pop out of nowhere, seeking whom they may devour.

Around here it's considered a sin straight from Hell to leave anything right side up so it holds water—bucket, plant pot, wheelbarrow—anything. The reason is simple: Mosquitoes breed in water. So if one leaves a wheelbarrow or empty pot outside when it rains, he had better empty out the water before the mosquitoes make it their 'hood. Around here we all must remove the source if we want to keep the mosquito population down.

On our journey to freedom, we must remove the sources of temptation in order to stay the course. And we must remove the sources at all costs. We must get that Internet filter. If not, cut the connection. Sound drastic? You bet. It's not worth the consequences. Trust me; I've seen them with far too many Christian, church-going guys. You can't afford the consequences.

So drive home from work a different way if your usual way home is by a sex shop that is calling your name. I can't put on the breastplate of righteousness if I keep giving in to the temptation that can be removed. I am not wearing the belt of truth if I tell myself I can't live without HBO or Cinemax. How easy it is to talk ourselves into keeping those things that bring in so much temptation. But it's just not worth the consequences of what sin brings.

Recently, I was visiting with a group of men who are the spiritual leaders in their church. They had the dreadful experience of dealing with their youth pastor who had committed adultery. One of these leaders was the youth pastor's best friend. These leaders told me of the night when they confronted him with their newfound and very unfortunate news of his sin. As they told me, they began to relive the experience, and their heads hung low. I could see on their faces the pain they felt inside. It was excruciating.

They told me the youth pastor had only one car, so his wife had to bring him to the confrontational meeting. Neither the youth pastor nor his wife knew that these leaders found out his sin. The wife dropped him off and went home. The senior pastor told me he watched out the window of his office as the youth pastor and his wife drove up. He said his heart sank as he knew the pain that was about to take place in that young couple's lives.

Since the youth pastor had only one car, he needed a ride home after that painful meeting. His best friend brought him home. He told me of that difficult ride in the car. Then, with tears, he told me that when he pulled into the driveway, he asked the youth pastor if he wanted him to go in the house with him as he broke the news to his wife of his unfaithfulness to her and to God. The youth pastor said, "No, I need to do this."

So the youth pastor got out of the car and walked toward the front door of his home, where his wife was inside cooking dinner in the kitchen. The best friend said he will never forget this "walk." He watched with a torn-apart heart as his friend opened the door, walked inside, and closed the door behind him. He said he could only imagine what would take place next as his cherished friend unveiled his dark secret of betrayal to his wife.

Remove all sources, men. It's just not worth that kind of "walk." This is what Jesus said in Matthew 5:29, "…if your right eye causes you to sin, pluck it out…" Perhaps many men ought to start wearing pirate patches to church! Or, better yet, many men need to understand that Jesus' point was to remove all sources of temptation. His context was committing adultery in the heart by lusting after other women.

Men, this youth pastor's dreadful walk to his front door started with viewing pornography. Remove all sources. It's simply not worth the consequences. You're wondering why I keep stating that, aren't you? Because it's too true. In fact, I'll type it again: It's simply not worth the consequences.

Invest in a reliable monitoring software, like Covenant Eyes, or do what the senior pastor of this fallen youth pastor did and disconnect the Internet to your computer. Eliminate the Internet browser on your smart phone, or purchase software for it. (Covenant Eyes has one for that, too.) You don't want to experience the consequences. They are terrible beyond comprehension. Remove all sources before it's too late.

I've thought of a few other possible sources you might need to think about removing.

1. The drive to work that takes you by stores that sell pornographic material. Go a different route.
2. The pretty girl who cuts your hair. Go to a male barber. (Or an ugly girl. Sorry, I had to say it).
3. The gas station that sells pornographic magazines. Go to a station that doesn't sell them.
4. The R-rated movies (and many PG-13 movies) in your collection that contain nudity. Burn 'em, don't sell 'em!
5. The Internet. Get monitoring or filtering software like Covenant Eyes, or cut off the connection.
6. Those lingerie magazines that come to your wife. Discontinue the subscription. (And don't tell me you like to read the articles.)
7. The smart phone on your hip. Disable the Internet browser, or get Covenant Eyes software for it.
8. The beach or neighborhood swimming pool. Just don't go.

Okay, I know what you're thinking. This looks like a list of rules to follow in order to be holy. In one way, it is, but these aren't rules for every man. An alcoholic who is trying to break the addiction shouldn't have a beer. A smoker who is trying to kick the habit shouldn't light up even one (because it's never just one). A man pursuing freedom in his thought-life shouldn't put himself in harm's way. These are only ideas that some need to follow.

My point is that in order to journey your way to freedom, there just might be some things that you need to avoid. Make a list of those things and share them with your 3. There just might be some sources to remove because the journey to freedom is accomplished by pursuing God's holiness.

Equip Yourself

Have you ever been hungry? I'm talking about *really* hungry? My wife and I have four kids. Our youngest right now is 8 months old. Katherine is a blue-eyed angel...unless she's hungry.

Occasionally, Melissa will be out with some friends or at the grocery store, and I'll be home caring for the kiddos. This usually involves giving them something to eat and watching a *VeggieTales* video. One time I fed my son, Jonathan, my two oldest daughters, Kristina and Caroline, but somehow forgot to feed Katherine. Let me tell you, it didn't take long before she reminded me that I had missed something very important. I had missed her mealtime! So I hurriedly mixed up the baby food and got her bottle ready, put her in her high chair, and fed her yummy mashed up peas and rice cereal, followed by her usual four ounces of formula. Then it happened. It always does. She finished eating and gave me one huge you-are-the-best-daddy-in-the-universe smile! She's right; I am. She was my angel again—the only angel that sports a green, mashed-peas-and-rice-cereal smile!

The truth is, she couldn't go on without food any longer. Her body, as small as it is, requires food more often than an adult's body does. Men, if we are to journey to freedom successfully, we need food. Anybody who knows anything knows you're supposed to pack food for a journey. However, many Christian men seem to forget that important fact. Men trek down the road missing something very important, and after a while they get famished. That's when it begins to set in—spiritual starvation. We just can't go any longer without the spiritual food.

God has provided a vast army of resources to help men like you and me to persevere in our journey to freedom. One of the things I must do daily is really something I'm not very fond of doing. I really don't like to read much. But I know that I have to if I want to continue learning.

For me, reading is like exercising. I don't like exercising much, either. But I know I have to if I want to continue to be healthy. I have found, though, that it's much easier for me to keep on an exercising schedule if I exercise with someone else. So my wife and I purchased a set of workout DVDs, and we are exercising in the morning before the kids get up. Reading, for me, comes much more easily when I am going through worthwhile books with other guys.

I enjoy participating in online book discussions with other guys. These usually consist of men going through some great books, usually one chapter at a time, and discussing them online at a community site's chatroom and forum. I can't tell you when I've seen better openness and honesty than these groups of men who are equipping themselves together by going through these books!

These guys are challenging one another, me especially, to continue their journey to freedom with great joy. We are realizing that living lives of purity occurs more easily when we are doing it together. And I've realized so many of these men have been starving for this spiritual nourishment. I also realize there so many other guys who are still starving. We need to equip ourselves, for the journey to freedom is accomplished through dependence upon God's resources.

Pick a Partner

This book is about men's journey to freedom. This journey cannot be accomplished alone. It's accomplished with the help of authentic fellowship with other men. I have given the biblical mandate for authentic fellowship and some practical how-to's. My prayer is that these things will inspire you to begin your journey, encourage you to continue on the path, and introduce you to the joy of Christ's freedom. I'm convinced authentic fellowship with other Christian men is a must and that it can provide the encouragement you need to live like you already are in Christ—freely. That's why every man needs his 70-12-3-1. Picking a partner involves these groups already discussed.

However, for some guys who have fallen so deep into addictive sin, they need more than just authentic fellowship with other guys. Picking a partner for them might mean finding a professional Christian counselor. Counseling for addictions, such as sex, alcohol, drugs, etc., is available just about everywhere. There are various degrees of counseling—from in-house that could last a few months to out-patient where the counselee can come and go based on appointments. Good, biblical counseling is actually a necessity for every believer, and God has provided some great Christian counselors that are helping thousands of men just like you. Talk to your pastor, or your 3, to help you find a professional Christian counselor, for the journey to freedom is accomplished by trusting God's provision.

CHAPTER EIGHT

THERE'S FREEDOM ON THE
OTHER SIDE

What do building programs, the color of carpet, worship music, and tornadoes have in common? They have all had a hand in splitting churches.

Several years ago the southern part of Alabama suffered many violent tornadoes that swept across the land. Ironically, many church buildings were destroyed. To make matters worse, it happened on a Sunday morning when church buildings were filled with worshippers.

There was one story where the church members were inside singing a hymn when a tornado hit. One of the ushers apparently wanted to peek outside (every church has one of these guys), so he opened the doors to the main auditorium and the wind blew them wide open. It took several men to close the doors, but before they were closed they saw the tornado lift their Sunday school building off the ground. The hymn they were singing at the time was "I'll Fly Away." No, I'm not kidding.

I live near Galveston, Texas. You've probably heard of this area since Hurricane Ike devastated the island of Galveston and many of the surrounding communities in 2008. A friend of mine is the pastor of a church on the island. His church had up to four feet of water inside. As I am writing this book one year later, they are still working on repairs to their buildings.

Tornadoes, hurricanes, fights over music, building programs— many things can devastate a church body. Those can be tough times, but none as tough as when an influential man in a church is caught in a sexual sin. To say that it devastates the people is an understatement. Most of them never really get over it. And, believe it or not, the ones who probably suffer the most (besides the husband, wife, and children, of course) are the spiritual leaders of the church. They find themselves torn between what to do with the sinning brother and how to protect their congregation. I have found that many church leaders do not know what to do when they are ambushed with a situation like this. It is a very, very tough event to endure with wisdom.

Many have asked how a Christian man can get so caught up in a sin like adultery or porn addiction or anything similar. I believe that if more churches had authentic fellowship among their men, fewer of them would fall into such sins. Far fewer. And I'm fully convinced there are many men in every church who are struggling with porn addiction, several of whom have already acted out their fantasies with other people. How do Christian men get this far?

I would like to entertain this and a few other questions in this chapter, but first I would like to share with you a story. Actually, I would like for a friend of mine to share with you his story. He's a brother in Christ who was once a worship leader at a large church in Alabama. His decisions almost ruined his life. They still could, if he's not careful. But so could your decisions and my decisions.

I have asked my friend, Greg, to share his story with you for many reasons. In this story, you will see a Christian man whose sex addiction began very early in age. You'll see the consequences of the lack of authentic fellowship. You will see the progression of temptation and sin. You will see—and probably feel, as I did—the pain of his shame and guilt. You will see the hurt he has caused others, as well as the hurt he received from others.

But you will also see the truth He learned about God's freedom: forgiveness, grace, mercy, acceptance, love, peace, and triumph. I ask that you read his story in one sitting, and then reread it in another sitting. Take personal notes regarding your thoughts, questions, and emotions as you read through Greg's story.

Many of the stories I've read over the years of Christian men falling into immorality have left harmful pictures in my mind, so Greg purposefully left out the gory details. Even I don't know those details. But he didn't sacrifice the reality of his sin in expressing some of the facts that took place. Here now, in chronological order, is Greg's story.

Greg's Story

January 6, 2009

I'm sitting at my desk and rereading the email. It had come the previous afternoon and I had read it then, but I hadn't really given it much thought. Now, as I read it again, a weight of realization hits me like a ton of bricks. This email is about me. It was sent to all the pastors from our executive pastor, and it said our normal Tuesday meeting was going to be cancelled because an issue had come up that was going to require his and the pastor's attention for all of the day.

As I read the email again, I know the issue is me. My mistake had resulted in what I feared it would, and I had been found out. My mind is racing at the speed of light. How can I spin this? Is there any way out? I know there isn't. What am I going to do? For the briefest second I'm thinking about jumping off an overpass. Ridiculous. I can't do that to my family, and besides, I'm too chicken to ever do anything like that. Slowly the truth settles in. I am caught. What's going to happen is going to happen. How did I get here?

1981

I don't remember exactly when, but I'm pretty sure I was about 11 years old when I began to experience the hormonal surge of puberty. I had always been pretty aware of sexuality, and always pretty curious, too. I can remember watching a show on public television when I was about 6 or 7 that talked about human sexuality. It described the process in very clinical terms, and there was a lot I didn't understand. But I definitely got the basics of how ⊠it⊠ worked. I wasn't obsessed with it yet, but I did think about it a lot.

Like I said, around age 11 things started changing, and I started becoming more preoccupied with sexual feelings. I discovered masturbation, and pretty much right off the bat that was something I was regularly doing. At first I don't think it was every day, but it was pretty often.

The thing about being 11 years old and experiencing sexual things for the first time is that you don't really know yet how to exercise discretion. I wasn't doing anything in the open, but apparently I wasn't too discrete because my mom somehow found out what I was doing. I grew up in a home where both my parents were Christians. We went to a conservative, Bible-teaching church, and I was exposed to great teaching from a very young age. I had a good grasp on knowing right from wrong, but I really don't remember thinking much about the morality of masturbation. That changed when I got some "instruction" about it one day. Listening to all the reasons why it was bad and sinful to do a thing like that, I knew two things already. First, I wasn't going to stop. I enjoyed it too much. Second, I was going to have to get better at hiding it.

What I didn't realize at the time was that a pattern of secrecy, shame, and addictive behavior was starting, and it would continue for almost 28 years.

1982-1989

The next few years were pretty normal for a pre-teen and young teenage boy. I had a normal life, went through normal things, and was generally happy and content. I still struggled with lust and masturbation, but thought for the most part that it was just something that all guys dealt with. I just knew I had to deal with it on my own.

In the eighties, and where I grew up, a boy had to go looking for pornography. It wasn't rampant. We didn't have adult bookstores in my hometown, and of course the Internet wasn't around yet. So I never had a constant stream of porn flowing into my life, but I got it whenever I could. I know had porn been as accessible then as it is now, I would have been drowning in it. I had plenty of conviction, guilt, and shame. I just had no self-control, and no one I could talk to about it.

All through high school I continued being the "good guy." I went to a Christian school and never got in trouble. I was a leader in my youth group. I sang in church. I dated a couple of good Christian girls and never went "too far." That was when people were watching. When it was just me, I was still masturbating. I was still exposing myself to porn whenever I could, occasionally buying my own magazines now instead of relying on my brother's stash.

Anytime I could get away with it, I'd rent movies with sexual content. And all the while I was feeling incredible guilt and shame. I knew God was watching, and I knew He wasn't pleased. But I also knew nothing was really going to change. I didn't have enough will power—I knew that. What I didn't know was all this behavior was having a devastating impact on my view of sex and on my future.

There were a few times I really thought about talking with someone, but who would it be? I could have talked with my youth pastor, but I was afraid that if I did that, my parents would find out. That wasn't going to happen, so rather than take the risk of letting someone in, I kept it to myself again.

1989-1991

The struggles I was dealing with didn't consciously consume every moment, or even every day. I was living my life, and enjoying a lot of it. God was very real to me, and I believed He was calling me to go into full-time ministry. After I graduated from high school I went to college at home. During that first year, I was chaperoning a youth retreat and spent a lot of time with the speaker, who was the recruiter at Southeastern Bible College in Birmingham, Alabama. By the end of the retreat I was convinced that Southeastern was the place for me. In the fall of 1989, I moved to Birmingham to go to Bible college.

During these years I behaved myself pretty well. My focus was on my study and on preparing for ministry. Even though I goofed off a lot, I was generally committed to the path I had chosen. I don't remember any porn during those years. I'm sure there was some; it just wasn't a time when it was an intense struggle. Of course I was still masturbating; by now that was so normal I rarely even thought about it. My conscience was being affected, and I didn't realize it.

In the spring of 1990, I started spending a lot of time with Stacey. We were already friends, but during that semester we both realized that our relationship was turning into more than a friendship. Since we started dating so close to the summer, and since we were going to be apart, I decided it would be best if we left ourselves free to date other people.

We realized soon into the summer that neither of us had any desire to date other people. We picked up our relationship when we got back to school in the fall, and by the next spring we were engaged.

Our engagement was 9½ months long. That is too long. I'm almost willing to say that it's too long for anyone. But it was definitely too long for us. We were both very affectionate, and we loved physical contact. Our relationship was already pretty physical by the time we got engaged, and during our engagement we didn't exercise much self-control. We looked for every opportunity we could to be alone, so we could enjoy intimacy with each other that wasn't supposed to be happening yet.

We spent a lot of time during our engagement feeling guilty and ashamed. We knew that we were doing wrong by how physical we were in our relationship. We knew each time we got closer and closer to having intercourse and would then stop, that our guilt would be stronger. But it wasn't just guilt.

Stacey was resenting me because I was failing to be the spiritual leader in our relationship. I was resenting her because she kept letting us get into the position where I'd fail. We would pray and try to do better, but the next time we'd end up right there again. We entered our marriage "technical" virgins, having done pretty much everything except intercourse. We didn't realize the impact this would have on our future.

That's the thing about our actions. What we so often fail to realize is that the impact of our actions is not limited to the place we are when we do them. My habit of masturbating contributed to my porn intake. My porn intake contributed to my preoccupation with sex. This preoccupation contributed to my behavior with Stacey. All of this contributed to a constantly growing sense of shame that I was a phony and a failure. I was not who everyone thought I was. I was not a "good Christian."

But when I would do these things, I'd temporarily forget about those shameful things. They made me feel good, and that was what I wanted. At some point during these years, my sexual acting out became an addiction. Masturbating wasn't just something I did, it was something I needed to do. Sexual gratification was something I had to have; otherwise I almost couldn't focus on other things in life. I was already in trouble, and I didn't know it yet.

1992-1996

Stacey and I were married on January 4, 1992. One of the things I was most looking forward to, like most guys, was having sex with her. But one of the reasons I was most looking forward to it was because I thought it was going to fix all of my other problems with sex. Once I was married, I could have wild, hot, sweaty, passionate movie sex with my wife all the time. I would never again need to masturbate. I would never again need to look at porn. All my fulfillment would be met because we would be having sex all the time, and it would be spectacular.

I was unprepared for the fact that reality doesn't live up to fantasy. That's why it's fantasy...it isn't real, or even close. All my exposure to sexual imagery over the years had created such a huge hunger for gratification, and along with that an unrealistic expectation of how sex was going to be. To put it mildly, it wasn't so hot right off the bat. It wasn't movie sex, and that's what I wanted.

Things got better, but it was a slow process. The first few years we fought a lot about sex. When a husband who has been experiencing gratification through improper means on a daily basis doesn't get his movie sex, things aren't always going to be peachy and happy. I almost immediately got back into frequent masturbating. Stacey became aware of it, and it devastated her. She felt betrayed, but also felt like my masturbating was a reflection on her failure to please me. We didn't really talk about it, other than for me to lie and tell her that I'd stop.

Once again I knew two things. First, I wasn't going to stop. And second, I had to do a better job of hiding it. Slowly, porn started to creep back in as well. I'd occasionally get my hands on a magazine or video. I was unfulfilled and unhappy, and by now I'd learned how to cover that (however temporarily) with sexual acting out. But just as it had always been, every streak of acting out was followed by an intense conviction over my sin, great remorse, and a commitment never to do it again.

It was also in these first couple of years of marriage when I first was really exposed to real live temptation. I began noticing and second-looking a lot, and foolishly letting my guard down lower and lower.

When I finished at Southeastern, we moved to Lake Charles, Louisiana, where I became a youth and music pastor. It was a great first stop in ministry; a good place to grow and learn and begin to put into practice a lot of what I'd learned in school. We had our first child while we were in Louisiana. We also got our first computer, and I got my first unfiltered exposure to the Internet. All of a sudden I didn't have to look for it anymore. It was always right there whenever I wanted it. Now my binges would expose me to a lot more I could feel guilty about.

The pastor in Lake Charles (Don Barrett) was, and still is, a great friend. He was a caring, compassionate person and a great father to his kids. I remember talking with him in his office one day about his relationship with his oldest son, Chad. Don talked about his conversations with Chad regarding growing up, dating, puberty, masturbation, and other things.

I was so jealous. I had never talked about things like that with my dad. I remember almost sharing with Don all the things with which I was struggling. But I didn't. By then I was convinced no one would understand. If I told, I'd be in trouble. I might even lose my job. No, I was just going to have to figure out how to fix this on my own. I often wonder how different the next 13 or 14 years would have been had I said something to Don that day.

1997-2002

We moved back to Birmingham in January of 1997. I had gotten pretty burned out at the previous church. It was a small, old, traditional church, and they had gotten weary of the changes to the music I was introducing. Support and participation faded, and I had become stressed and frustrated much of the time. These emotions of mine fed my porn intake, and my porn intake fueled these emotions even further. In a way, I thought (foolishly) that a change of scenery would help the problem. If I could just get away from the environment where I was struggling, I'd be able to escape the constant temptation. But temptation follows you wherever you go. And secret temptation can keep an extremely low profile, settling itself comfortably into whatever new setting you find.

Being back in Birmingham was comfortable and fun. I was working at Southeastern and having an impact on students. It was a different kind of ministry, and I liked it. I had needed a break from the week-in, week-out work of church music ministry, and I especially liked the personal relationships I was forming with the students. I was even helping many of them with their own struggles, all the while holding on to my own.

Stacey and I were plugging along in our marriage, getting along but settling for far less than we should have. We simply didn't know what we were missing. We'd never experienced real intimacy or complete honesty. We both had things we were disappointed about, but we adjusted our expectations and moved on.

I had begun to feel my disappointing sexual experiences entitled me to seek fulfillment through other means. I knew this wasn't really true, but it made it easier to live with the porn and masturbating. I had gotten to a point where I was looking for any and every opportunity to indulge myself. Most every time Stacey would be out of town overnight, or even for an evening, I'd find a way (often planning in advance) to get a sexually explicit movie to watch, or would spend hours online looking at porn and masturbating.

The crazy thing was, every time I did it, I'd feel terrible afterward. It got to a point where I stopped even convincing myself that it would be fulfilling. I knew there would be terrible remorse, but I did it anyway. Stacey suspected that I was masturbating every time she was gone, and she was right. What she didn't know was where it was heading was far worse and deeper than she imagined.

I was pretty sure by this point that I was addicted to sex. I even had started researching sex addiction on the Internet. Not to the point where I'd follow through and get help, mind you, but just enough to convince myself that I was trying to do something.

One of these times I was actually going to fix myself. Stacey found a search inquiry I did one time when she was typing some other search and the auto-complete feature popped up, "How do I know if I'm addicted to sex?" She asked me about it, and I lied. By now I was a good enough liar to convince her to drop it, even though doubts remained in her mind.

In early 1998, I was hired as Worship Pastor at a church in Birmingham. It started out part-time, but after about a year, I left Southeastern and was working full-time at the church. This church was different than the one in Lake Charles. It was a young church, more progressive and open to the type of music I enjoyed and did well.

The first few years went really well, and I was growing and developing as a pastor and as a musician. But all the while, there were two conflicting stories going on in my life. There was what everyone else saw, and there was what only God and I knew. And I didn't really even talk much with Him about it because I knew He wasn't pleased with my failure. It was better just to try harder, so I thought. Then I could go to Him once I had a little success under my belt.

After a few years at the church, the stress was growing. I found myself looking at porn any chance I could, and at more explicit, hardcore porn, too. It was arousing, and at the same time all of it was disgusting. I honestly wanted to be free, but I felt trapped. It was a big enough struggle now that I "knew" I couldn't tell anyone. Surely they'd fire me if they knew. Stacey would never understand.

Managing it on my own wasn't working, but what other choice did I have? I'd have to try harder. And as usual, it would work for a while. But the cycle was getting shorter every time, and the period of acting out was getting longer. I was in trouble, and I knew it.

At some point in late 2002, I found my thoughts turning toward wondering what it would be like to act out sexually with someone else. I convinced myself that it was something I would never do, and that made it easier to dwell on it. Wondering how I would do it led me to decide that maybe a sensual massage would be the most harmless way. After all, a massage is a perfectly legitimate thing to have. Maybe I'd just go for a regular one and see what happened. Maybe I'd get a sensual massage but nothing sensual would actually happen.

By the end of my mental conversation with myself, it made total sense to go. It would be anonymous, uncomplicated, and "clinical." In a way it would be "therapeutic." My pattern of deceit had developed into a strong pattern of self-deceit as well, and I convinced myself to a point where I made the decision to go for it.

I will always remember the drive home from my first sensual massage. I remember saying to myself, "I've just committed adultery." No, I hadn't had an affair, and I hadn't had sexual intercourse, but I'd taken part in sexual activity outside of my marriage, and I knew a huge line had just been crossed. I hated myself. I could not believe how far I'd let things go. And no one was going to ever find out.

2003-2008

After that, my conviction led to a pretty intense period of good behavior. I felt like I had turned away from my sin, and I'd never do it again. But slowly, like every time before, my willpower melted away.

I took a trip to Los Angeles—to a worship conference of all things—in the summer of 2003. During the preparations for the trip, I made an appointment for a sensual massage that I would have while I was there. My manipulative mind even planned it to be at the beginning of the trip. I knew that I'd feel guilty about it, would repent, go to the conference, and have a meaningful time being restored in my walk. It was the pinnacle of selfishness, and I had myself convinced otherwise.

Of course, I was right. Guilt and shame followed, and I did my ritual of repentance at the conference, feeling like it was a genuine step toward healing. What it was, though, was a fix. I was using God's forgiveness to ease my guilty conscience until the next time. And by now I knew there would be a next time.

It's hard to describe how a Christian man who honestly and earnestly desires to serve God can degrade to this point. How did I live with myself? How could I sustain a life of such utter dishonesty and deceit? The way I managed was through intense and strict compartmentalization. When I was acting out, that was one person—not really *me*—and when I was done with that behavior, the door to that room in my life was tightly shut.

When I was leading worship, I meant it. I meant every bit of it. While I would lead, I usually prevented myself from thinking about what I had done; and anytime those thoughts crept in, I'd tell myself to focus on grace. I had no idea what grace was. It became a hall pass, allowing me to do whatever I wanted to do. My concept of grace left out the cost of Christ's sacrifice and became a cheap –do-over– to ease my guilty conscience.

All the while, the real me knew deep down inside this stuff wasn't going to be able to go on forever. I knew I was getting out of control. Over time the gaps between incidents of acting out shortened. Eventually my activity became more involved and more frequent. I couldn't understand it. I didn't enjoy what I was doing. Each time I went to act out, my conscience would scream at me, "Don't go!" As I'd get closer to the place where I was going, I'd sense, "It's not too late…turn around!" But somehow, I continued.

Of course I had a choice, but somehow it felt as if I didn't. I was way past the point of thinking my actions would make me feel better. I knew any good feelings would be far overshadowed by shame. But for some reason, each time I continued.

In order to make it work, to be able to go on living with myself, I had created a whole different identity to slip into when I was acting out. If I could compartmentalize to the extent of actually becoming someone else, then maybe the other times wouldn't feel so guilty. For a while it worked, but just like every other step downhill I'd taken, it didn't take long before conviction became louder than the lie I was telling myself.

I was out of control, and I knew it. Long ago, my prayers were that I'd never do it again. By this time, they had been replaced by prayers that I would be caught. They weren't noble prayers, like it may sound. Somehow I felt if I prayed that I'd get caught, maybe instead God would respect my "honesty" and just fix me, and no one would have to know what I'd done.

What a joke.

The fall of 2008 was a period of escalation that was faster and more intense than any so far. I was acting out more and more frequently, and my behavior was getting riskier. I was using email as a way of communication and scheduling hookups, and was beginning to come close to breaking my own rule about keeping it anonymous and free of anything personal. I didn't realize it, but I was reaching a breaking point. Something was going to happen one way or another.

I've heard it said that addicts end up in one of three places: recovery, prison, or the grave. I believe that I was headed toward one of the latter options. I occasionally thought (and would then suppress the thought) that one day I'd find out I had contracted HIV. And all the time, I was still sleeping with my wife, putting her at the same risk time and time again. It's a level of selfishness and insanity I believe I'll probably never fully understand.

January 6-13, 2009

Well, this brings me back to where I began this story.

Sometime around New Year's Eve or New Year's Day, everything changed. I sent an email to someone with whom I'd acted out. But instead of sending it using the dummy email address I'd created for my false identity, I accidentally sent it using my church account. So now my real identity was out there, and the consequences were out of my hands.

I didn't have to wait long. It was the next Monday, January 5, that I received the email from the executive pastor. I read the email and, strangely, didn't think anything about it. I went home after work, and then came in the next morning planning to use the time created by our cancelled meeting to work on some long-range planning for the spring and summer. As I settled into my desk, I reread the email, and all of a sudden it hit me.

"A situation has come up…"

"…will require our immediate attention…"

"…will take the entire day…"

They knew. Somehow they found out. It was over. The truth was about to come out. But the addict in me was still alive and kicking. I tried to think through all the emails I'd sent and remember what information they might have. I tried to decide what I would have to admit to, and what I could deny. I thought of all that I'd done that was not even mentioned in the emails. I knew this was going to be bad, but maybe it was still manageable. Maybe I could limit the damage.

I called Stacey and asked her to swing by the office when she was done. I tried to sound upbeat, so as not to let her know on the phone that anything was wrong. I needed more time to decide how and what I was going to tell her. When she got to the office, I got into the van with her and she immediately knew something was wrong.

I drove us to a nearby church parking lot and began to tell her what I had decided she needed to know. I admitted to the list of things I had decided she could handle, keeping a lot of the truth secret still.

Stacey was devastated. She screamed and cried and didn't understand, and I wondered what was coming for us. I contacted the executive pastor, and we went to meet with him and the pastor. I retold the same story to them, full of half-truths. They said the elders were meeting that evening to decide what needed to happen.

Later that day I met with the men in my accountability group. These were guys with whom I'd met for almost ten years, and with whom I'd never been truly honest or vulnerable about my struggles. They didn't know how to handle it. They had great intentions to help walk with me through a recovery and restoration process, but none of us knew what that was going to look like. And as far as I knew, none of these guys had a clue how to relate to what I'd done or struggled with over two thirds of my life.

The next morning I met with the pastor, executive pastor, and chairman of our elders. They let me know the elders had decided to ask for my resignation, which I immediately gave. I was told the church was going to help us by setting us up with a counselor (and paying for it), and they would continue to pay my salary and keep me on insurance for three months while I searched for another job.

The next day we met with our counselor, Becky, for the first time. Right off the bat, she was wonderful—very calming and encouraging, and she helped to put things in immediate perspective. She answered many of our initial questions. Yes, this is extremely common. No, I'm not the only one. She confirmed my suspicions that I was a sex addict, but now we were beginning to understand exactly what that meant. There was a lot of pain in my life that hadn't been dealt with, and I had been using sexual acting out to try to fix it. We met with Becky twice this first week. Stacey and I were still in shock, but left her office feeling hopeful.

But still I was holding back. As Stacey and I sat in Becky's office, I can remember wondering if she was buying that what I admitted to was everything there was to know. After all, she was a professional counselor. She's trained and experienced at spotting when people are lying or holding back. But by this time, I was a professional liar, or at least semi-pro. I felt I could convince her, just like I believed I had convinced Stacey and all the others so far. And I believed that it wouldn't matter anyway. What she was going to share with us would be the same whether I admitted some or all, right? I'd just privately apply her counsel to the still-secret stuff I was hiding.

In the meantime, good things were already starting to happen. The counseling was teaching me great new things that later I'd be able to apply to the entirety of my experience. Even though I hadn't come clean about everything, it felt good to know that general knowledge of what I'd been hiding was out, and healing was underway. Still, I was playing the rationalizing game with myself and everyone else, trying to keep at least part of my secret still secret.

Looking back, it's easy to see the foolishness of this way of thinking. I believed God had brought my secret out into the open. Did I honestly believe He was going to settle for a half-hearted acknowledgement? Whether I believed it or not, He wasn't going to let it go. I didn't realize it, but the guys in the accountability group were having a hard time buying my story that a lot of the content of the emails was just fantasy that I'd made up. They wanted to somehow be sure that everything was out on the table. They wanted to put their detective caps on and get to the bottom of it.

They didn't know what they were doing. They were plowing through like bulls in a china shop. But God was using them. He was breaking me down. I still hung on to the fact that there wasn't any way to prove that anything more than what I'd already admitted to had taken place.

The first Sunday after my resignation, January 11, we had decided to go to worship at another church we had attended several years before. That morning, though, we had a lot of time to spend at home since the service didn't begin until 11:00. I knew our pastor was going to read a statement acknowledging my resignation, and my former assistant texted me when it had been done in the first service. I had a time of mourning for what I had lost, weeping in my bedroom by myself.

When we went to worship that morning, it was an amazing healing experience for both Stacey and me. Many of the songs we sang were the same songs we had sung the last week (my last Sunday, as it turned out) at our church. We both cried a lot during the service. Toward the end of the service there were some baptisms, and one of them was a woman who shared her testimony through a video. In the video she shared that she had done things that had put her marriage and even her life at risk.

One morning her husband had come to her and told her he knew what she had done, he wasn't going anywhere, and if she ran he would run after her. Stacey wept as she listened. This was her heart and what she was already doing. I thought about how I was going to move on while I was still keeping secrets.

The next day I talked with one of the guys in the accountability group. He told me one of the other guys in the group was planning to check out my story. Scott and Stephanie, some close friends who had been walking through this with us since the first day, were at our house for dinner that night. Over dinner, while I was trying to force down some food, the other three were complaining about what the guys in my accountability group were doing.

They talked about how ludicrous it was that I would admit to some of the things but not to all of them. What would I have to gain? With every new thing they said, I felt like I was dying a little bit more inside. I wasn't going to be able to do this much longer. God wasn't going to let me keep it secret.

At some point during the conversation it became obvious to Scott and Stephanie that something was happening. Stacey had asked me if something I had denied was true, and something about my answer made her question me.

Our friends left the room, and Stacey asked me the question again. Again I denied it, but we both knew it was a pitiful attempt.

Then Stacey looked at me and said, "I want you to tell me what you did. I'm not going anywhere. And if you run away, I'm running after you." For the first time I could remember, I believed that if she knew the truth, maybe she would still love me. Maybe she wouldn't go anywhere. It was possible for someone to know everything about me and not reject me.

Once again she asked if I had done what I had previously denied. This time I couldn't deny it, so I just stayed silent. That was answer enough.

The next few moments were a blur. At some point, I fell apart. I was on the floor, balled up, weeping and moaning, and I honestly felt like I was going to die. I can remember crying, "Oh, my God... oh, my God...oh, my God" over and over again. Years of pent up secrets and emotions felt like they were pouring out of me. It felt as if I had been possessed, and all the evil was being painfully pulled out. During this time, Scott came back into the room and sat with me while Stacey went to call our counselor. She told her that everything had come out. Becky reassured Stacey that this was not unexpected, it was how it usually happened, and she would see us the next morning.

In the meantime Scott started helping me come up with a timeline of all my acting out. From the smallest incident to the most intense things I had done, it was a long list. This represented years of secretive, addictive acting out. Over the next day, as anything came to mind, I immediately told Stacey about it as part of the purging process I was going through.

After awhile, Scott went home and Stacey and I stayed up talking until early morning. It was strange. After the intensity of my disclosure, we slowly were transitioning to calmly talking about things. I don't think either of us really understood what was happening. But I do remember how good it felt to know everything was really out now, and I wasn't –in trouble– with God or anyone else. Sure, there were going to be consequences, and I didn't know fully what they were going to be, but the main one—the loss of my job and the public knowledge that I'd failed—had already been done. I felt a huge weight lifted.

The next day was good, although more reality set in. We saw Becky again, and she helped me understand the road ahead was a long one. But she was very encouraging, too—letting me know it was very common for things to come out the way they had. She emphasized how critical it was to be completely and fully honest with my disclosure to Stacey. All throughout the day I continued to share things as they came to mind.

The reality came in a heavy dose later that day when we had to go take an HIV test at the health department. I had cheated with people I didn't know and had to make sure I hadn't caught anything. Sitting in the waiting room next to Stacey brought a new realization that I had not only put our marriage at risk, but both our lives as well. My addiction—and the choices that I made from it—had led me to places about which I've heard others talk. I'd done things I thought I'd never do and gone places I never thought I'd go.

My selfishness had jeopardized my entire family. And yet, along with the heaviness of this realization came a continuing feeling of freedom. I didn't have words for it yet, but now I know I was starting to understand that God wasn't angry with me. I believe that since I'd been a Christian for so long, and since I'd struggled badly with sexual sin for so long as well, that I made myself see God as being very distant. Surely He was disappointed in me. I think for a long time I tried to keep a distance between God and me. That was starting to change.

I began the work of recovery. Along with counseling, Becky gave me a workbook to go through. She also recommended I join a group of other addicts for support and accountability. I began attending a group on Monday nights, where I've met several men who are becoming good friends as we work through recovery together. I also reconnected with a couple of guys I already knew, but never knew that we shared the same struggles.

February 2009...

The time since that week in January has been extraordinary. God has done incredible work in my life, in Stacey's life, and in our family. So much of it has come through relationships that have begun or been reestablished because of my experience.

One of the first people I wanted to talk with was Kelly Stephenson. Kelly was a friend from years ago when we'd attended the church we now attend again. He had also been a worship pastor and had lost his job when the truth about his own addiction came out. I met with Kelly and shared my story with him. He told me his as well, and by the end of our first lunch together he agreed to become my sponsor as I walked through recovery.

Kelly has been a tremendous support—always speaking encouragement to me and pointing out areas where I need to be cautious. He also invited me to come sing with his choir on Easter Sunday. It was amazing to have someone who knew everything about me tell me God could—and still wanted to—use me.

Some new friends God has brought to Stacey and me are Tal and Teresa Prince. One of the men in my Monday night group told me about a church called Tapestry of Hope that meets on Sunday nights. Becky had already told me about Tapestry in one of our counseling sessions. And Kelly had mentioned it, too; he had helped start it. I figured with all of these mentions of Tapestry of Hope coming in rapid-fire, it might be something we ought to check out.

I had lunch with Tal and my friend from the group, and Tal was amazing. He was so accepting, so supportive; it was just more of what I'd been experiencing with Becky, Kelly, and of course Stacey. This was something so new…having people who knew the real me but still wanted to hang around!

When we visited Tapestry we found that there were other people we knew who attended there. And Stacey knew Teresa from when our daughters were in the same pre-K class a few years prior. God used this new friendship to really help lock in my understanding of His acceptance of me despite my failure. Tapestry was the first place where I sang after all my stuff came out.

I had heard a song at church on a Sunday morning called *Not Guilty Anymore*, and had bought the CD. I recommended it on my Facebook page, and after Tal heard it, he asked me to sing the song at Tapestry. I can't describe the feeling I had. I guess I had felt leading music and worship was something I had given up, or at least wouldn't be able to do for a long time. Tal's invitation—coming from someone who knew everything I had done—really communicated God's love and forgiveness in a tangible way to me.

I got to reconnect with another old friend, someone I had met over fifteen years earlier but with whom I had not kept up. He and I used to run together, and we started running again when we could. He suggested I read and listen to Steve Brown, a Christian radio host and author. I downloaded and listened to an entire course he taught on grace in the church. It has been an amazing way to take a fresh look at God's grace.

Steve was the first person to tell me that God wasn't angry with me anymore, and was, in fact, quite fond of me because of what Christ did.

All these friendships, and the teaching I was exposing myself to now, were so helpful in walking through the early days of my recovery. Not everything was terrific. Not all our friendships stayed intact. We did not remain at the church where I'd served for over a decade. After making this decision, we committed to become more involved at the church we were attending. It's a large church, and in order for us to build any real relationships we were going to have to plug into a small group. The kids had already begun to get comfortable with the kid's and youth ministries, so one night we looked over the long list of adult small groups.

We found a new group listed that was made up of couples in their 30s and 40s, so we decided to try it. The first Sunday we visited we wondered what we'd gotten ourselves into. The group was much smaller than we were expecting; we'd hoped for a little anonymity right off the bat, but we stayed anyway. Everyone in the group was very warm and welcoming, but asked the questions one would expect them to ask of newcomers. Were we new to Birmingham? Where did we attend church before we came here? With every question, it became more obvious we were either going to have to hide what was going on, or go ahead and dive into letting people know some of that with which we'd been dealing.

We shared that I had been on staff at a church, and that I'd lost my job because of a moral failure. It was awkward, but probably more for me than for anyone else. The people in the group were very gracious and loving in their responses, and we felt really good about having shared what we did.

Over the next few weeks we found out we were not the only ones in our group who had walked through the consequences of adultery. We were feeling more at home in this group than with many of the people we'd gone to church with for more than a decade. Here was a group of people who really wanted to be close, in authentic and transparent relationships with one another. It was certainly not perfect, but we were all pursuing the right things, and we felt sure that God had led us here.

Now that the newness of the experience was wearing off and reality was settling in, situations have changed. I got a job at a Chick-fil-A, working over 50 hours each week, earning about half of what I was making at the church. The severance pay ended, and now we're in a place where we're unsure of how all our obligations will be met each month.

But in the midst of the uncertainty, there are a lot of things that are certain. God continues to reaffirm His love for us through one another, through His Word, and through many other relationships. He's providing opportunities for me to begin serving through music again, in safe and healthy environments. And He's already shown us several times, through the unexpected kindness and generosity of friends, that He will take care of us and meet our needs. There are options for other, better jobs that I'm pursuing, and I know that as I seek and ask for wisdom, He'll provide that too.

So here we are, less than a year into a brand new life. I don't know what things are going to look like in a week or month or year, but I do have the confidence we're going to be okay. I know what I'm capable of, and I know I could fall again, but I'm committed to a new way of living—with truth and transparency—and I believe God has led me to and will keep me in a life of purity.

What to Do Next?

Did you read Greg's story twice? Did you take some personal notes? Did you think I was kidding? Do it now.

How Can a Christian Man Get This Far?

What prevents a man from falling flat on his face? The very next step. Keep walking. Persevere. What should a man do when he does fall? Get back up. God's mercy and forgiveness never run dry. But what happens when a Christian man forgets these things?

Christian men sin. The Apostle Paul wrote to Christian people (the Corinthians) who were sinning just as badly as Greg did, if not worse, and called for discipline and repentance. The author of Hebrews wrote to Christians, warning them to keep the faith and not give up. James describes the process of sin, how it spirals downward toward death. He wrote his book to Christians, too.

While the Bible is clear that justification *declares* us righteous, it is also clear the justification doesn't *make* us righteous. And the Bible is clear that we can never lose that which we have never earned—our salvation is held by God, not by us (Eph. 2:8-9; Jn. 10:27-30). If Christians can't sin the way Greg did, then a lot of men are in deep trouble because Jesus said for a man to even look upon a woman with lust, he has committed adultery with her. If Christian men can't sin as much as Greg did, then how much is too much? And who is the one to say when too much is too much? We really start swimming in a sea of subjectivity here, don't we? The truth is, Christian men sin. So do Christian women and boys and girls.

You read how Greg fell deeper and deeper into his sin. So do gossipers. And backbiters. And haters. The difference is the Church doesn't frown so much upon those types of sins like we do with sexual sins. Yet I once saw firsthand what gossip did to one local church. It split it. This same church experienced a small exodus when one of the ministers had an affair years before that. However, when gossip got its foot in the front door, it wasn't long before the church was split in half. I saw it with my own eyes—half the church literally fell off and spread across the city. But we don't punish those who gossip like we do those who sin sexually. Perhaps we should. Or perhaps we ought to think more along the topic of grace balanced with truth. You know, just like Jesus did.

My point is Christian men can fall into deep sins of any kind. Lust, covetousness, idolatry, and adultery—we can all fall into any of these very deeply. Many Christian men are there already. If a man trusts in Jesus as his Savior, the man is going to heaven. But his salvation does not guarantee he will not commit sexual sins. This concerns me because I've known pastors and other church leaders who have told Christian men who were struggling with sex addictions that they were not truly saved. They say things like, "Real Christians don't do that."

My friends, how can a Christian man ever find freedom in his life if he's always wondering whether or not he is saved? John 5:24 tells us that we can *know* we are saved. It doesn't say we *hope* to be or we *may* be. Perhaps instead of asking how a Christian man can get this far, we should be asking how we can get those Christian men back.

That's what this book is all about. Authentic fellowship leads men to freedom. There are a few points I'd like to bring out regarding Greg's story. First, *the consequences of the lack of authentic fellowship among men can be severe.* Greg did not have authentic fellowship with other men. He wishes he had. He even stated that if he had opened up to one man, he may very well have avoided the turmoil of sin's destruction. His words to men today are simple: Authentic fellowship is not an option—it's a must.

Second, *sex addiction can start very early in age.* Greg's sex addiction seemed to have started with a small seed of curiosity when he was only 11 years old. Brothers, I've got a 10-year-old son at home. I don't want my son to experience what my friend, Greg, experienced. That's why Jonathan and I talk very openly about these things. Oh, we haven't talked about everything yet. But he knows about the birds and the bees now. I had that talk with him.

And sometime over the next year or two, I'll have the talk with him about masturbation, about lust, and about purity. Dads, you only have your sons and daughters for a certain length of time. Believe it or not, it's not a long time. Statistics are constantly coming out stating that sexual experimentation among kids is beginning earlier and earlier in age. Teachers are noticing these issues with elementary-aged kids. Talk to your kids. Be open with them. When they reach the age when they begin asking questions, share the truth with them. Share with them the struggles you've had. That will help your sons realize you are not God, and you are on your journey to freedom, and you will walk with your sons as they pursue purity in their lives.

Third, *sound doctrine alone taught in your church will not prevent you, or your sons and daughters, from any kind of addictions.* Remember how Greg said he grew up knowing right from wrong because his church taught great sound doctrine? Before I started pastoring at Faith Bible, I was a youth pastor for thirteen years. The few churches where I served each had sound teaching from the pulpit and in the Sunday school classes. Yet each of these had many men who struggled intensely with various addictions. I counseled countless moms and dads regarding their teenage sons and daughters who messed around with sex, drugs, alcohol, and other forms of addiction. Sound doctrine is vital to the health of a church, but only when it is combined with the knowledge of how to apply it in daily practice. That knowledge is best applied in the form of authentic fellowship.

Fourth, *one ought not count on the changing of his environment to remove the temptation.* I was hired to be youth pastor of a church several years ago, and as soon as I got there, the chairman of the elder board called me to let me know that he and his family were moving. He wanted to assure me that I was not the reason for their move, which I was quite thankful to know. But then he told me the reason. I was hurt for him when he said his son was wrapped up in drugs, and he wanted to move to another town to get his son away from the temptation.

Unfortunately, his son found another source for the drugs. Changing your environment will not necessarily remove the temptation. It may for some rare cases, but not for most. It may cause a break for a while, but the temptation doesn't always come from the world around you. Most of the time it comes from your own desires (see James 1:14). Starting off new somewhere else seems quite appealing for the desperate and hurting, but it usually doesn't solve the problem.

Number five is for you single guys. Are you ready for this? *Marriage will not solve your lust problems.* If it did, there wouldn't be adultery. Have you ever thought of that? Wives wouldn't leave their husbands because of their addiction to porn. Wives wouldn't be hurt to know their husbands think about other women when they masturbate. In fact, most times marriage irritates the lust problem. The reason is, as you read in Greg's story, because men who view porn expect those same actions to be performed during intimacy with their wives. But that's not reality. And expecting your future wife to act the way the women on the computer screen act will be torture for your bride.

Comparing your wife with trashy women is torture. It destroys her self-esteem. Believe it or not, all women find some kind of fault with their bodies. She could be Miss America, but she'll find something she doesn't like about her body. We guys brag about our gut hanging over our belts, but women aren't quite like that. Comparing her to someone else, especially a porn star, will seriously aggravate her fault-finding. Not to mention it's just an insensitive thing to do.

Depending on her personality, a wife may follow your wishes just to please you, even though she is very uncomfortable with it. Or she may pull away from you because she can never please you. What's worse is your future wife may just seek her affirmation elsewhere.

Sixth, *pray for your pastors and leaders.* Obviously, pray for all the men in your church, but don't forget your pastors in your daily prayers. Pray for their protection from evil and their endurance in temptation. And guys, take your pastor to the golf course and ask him how his thought-life is. He battles the same temptations you do. Your pastor needs his own 12-3-1.

Did you know most pastors feel they can't share their struggles with anyone among their congregation? There's the fear they would lose their reputation, credibility, or even their jobs. I've had many pastors tell me this very thing. Your pastors need to know you view them as eing just as human as you are. Your pastors need your support, your grace, your mercy, and your nonjudgmental ear. Pray for your pastors and be authentic with them. Perhaps you might be the one with whom he becomes authentic, too.

Seventh, *it's better to confess your small sins to someone now rather than wait until they grow.* All sins are damaging, but sins are like bad weeds. They grow out of hand if not dealt with soon. We live in a parsonage (a house provided by the church for the pastor and his family) next to our church. The property we live on is about seven acres of land. It's a great place for our kids and dog to run and play. And it's a lot of fun to cut the grass! No, I'm not kidding. When it's time to cut the grass, I open up the brown shed in the back, insert the key into the ignition, and start up The Tank.

I feel like a real man on The Tank. It's a zero-turn-radius mower with a sixty-inch wide cutting base. This thing has major cutting power and lots of speed! (I even popped a wheelie on it once, but don't tell my elders.) I love cutting the grass because I love riding on

The Tank. But I hate edging. None of us around here really likes to edge. That's why Chris, one of my good friends who's also an elder at our church, sprays Roundup all around the property. We hate to edge—at least I do—because if we let it go too long, it gets very out of hand. The grass and weeds grow all into the chain-link fences, making it headache to clean up. I hate it! In fact, I need some Tylenol just thinking about it. So we Roundup the whole place.

Sin is kind of like that, don't you think? I'm convinced it's much better to just Roundup the sin in my life by sharing these struggles with my 3. If I don't, my sin can easily grow way out of hand, growing all into other areas of my life. That can be a headache to clean up. It is for Greg, and it could be for you and me, too.

Eighth, *be sure your sins will find you out.* God said it, not me. He said it in Numbers 32:23. It applied to the Israelites then, and it applies to us today. We can't get away with our sins. The longer we keep our sins a secret, the more we'll have to keep being deceptive. The more we are deceptive, the more burdens we are carrying. After a while, those burdens just get too heavy for us to keep carrying, and the weight of our burdens becomes far beyond our capacity to carry them.

This is precisely why Greg, and many other men, wanted to get caught. The lie they told themselves was it would be better for them to keep up the deception than to tell someone and remove the burden. But those burdens begin to crush bone and scrape skin. Just ask Greg. No one wants that kind of pain. If you're keeping your sins secret, you can count on them coming out somehow, somewhere.

Nine, *there's freedom on the other side.* Men, this is it. This is the clincher. Yes, there are consequences to our sin. Yes, those consequences hurt. They are supposed to hurt. But freedom never comes without a cost. If you get a speeding ticket, you are no longer free. You are legally bound to either show up in court or pay your fine. That's the deal. Those are the consequences for breaking the law. If you are dabbling with addictive sin—such as sexual sins, drug or alcohol abuse, working too much and neglecting your family, or being obsessed with money—confess that sin to God and to your 12-3-1. Stop lying to yourself. You can't handle this alone, and you know it. You simply cannot conquer this by yourself. Authentic fellowship opens the door to freedom. It's waiting for you just on the other side. It's calling your name, pleading for you to come.

Freedom offers a life of love, joy, peace, patience, kindness, goodness, faithfulness, gentleness, and self-control (Gal. 5:22-23). The ball is in your court. It's your move. Make it.

CHAPTER NINE

DON'T FORGET THE OTHERS

Wow! We're already in the last chapter. I certainly hope you have enjoyed reading this as much as I have enjoyed writing it. To tell you the truth, I've learned quite a bit with this project. One thing I've learned is that I can get so excited about a project that I'll leave behind all my other duties. You see, I'm a husband, a dad, and a director of an evangelistic ministry. As important as getting this book finished and sent off to the publishers is, those "other things" are even more important to me. Nope, I mustn't forget about those "other things." This reminds me of a story.

Imagine for a moment you belong to someone else. Your body belongs to someone else. Even your very breath belongs to someone else. Now imagine your skin color is black and you live in the 1800's. You work six days each week to make someone else rich. The idea of freedom is a fleeting thought. You wouldn't ever expect to taste it. Then, one morning as you work the fields, you overhear your fellow slaves speak of something called the Underground Railroad.

Harriet Tubman once heard whispers of the Underground Railroad. She was born a slave on a Maryland plantation around the year 1820. Her real name was Araminta Ross, but everyone started calling her Harriet after her mother.

Growing up on the plantation was difficult, to say the least, especially during these trying years when the plantation where Harriet worked was falling on hard times. In 1844, Harriet met and married a free black man named John Tubman. She told her husband that she wanted to run away to be free, but her husband said if she tried it, he would tell her master. Freedom for a black person during those days was not easy, but Harriet didn't give up her hope of a life of freedom.

When she heard about this "underground railroad," it didn't take long to make her move. In 1849, she escaped as a slave and made herself free. She knew the woods well, and she only traveled at night. This "underground railroad," as it was called, consisted of several "stations" along the way toward the north. As she reached each station, she was told where to go next.

Soon, she made her way to Pennsylvania, and she was finally free. She tasted it, felt it, and cherished it! No more could a slave master rule over her. Freedom was so much more than she could ever imagine. However, something still burned within Harriet's heart. Faces of slaves she knew back on the plantation were etched in her mind. She just couldn't forget about the others.

So instead of enjoying her freedom alone, Harriet went back to the south to free as many slaves as she could. During the next few years, she acquired names like "Moses" and "General Tubman" due to her bravery and perseverance in freeing so many slaves. In fact, throughout her lifetime, she saved over 300 slaves.[10]

I'd like to finish this book with this thought: Don't forget about "the others." That's what Paul said in Galatians 6:2: "Bear one another's burdens." When you begin to taste the freedom of Christ by gaining your 70-12-3-1, by putting on the armor of God, and by PREParing yourself for battle, don't forget about the man who sits in the pew behind you on Sunday morning. You know who I'm talking about. He's the guy you met once, but barely remember his name.

A champion for authentic fellowship doesn't forget about the others. He doesn't leave behind those on the fringe. Harriet didn't forget about them. Her heart burned as she pictured their faces in her mind. Perhaps you should pray that God would etch the faces of men of your church into your mind, to give you the same burning passion in your heart for people that Jesus has—that Harriet had.

It's time for the Church to regain this phenomenal thing called fellowship. It's time for men to become what we are called to become, the spiritual leaders of our homes and churches, knowing now this will occur when we journey to freedom *together*. It's time for someone in your church to champion the cause of authentic fellowship. For the longer we wait, more and more men will fall. Yes, enjoy the freedom Christ has for you. Taste it! Bask in it! Never go back to what you were—a slave to your sin. That's what this book is all about. But share His grace with others. Shine His love. Spread His freedom. Don't forget about the others on your journey to freedom, for the journey is never to be taken alone.

Finishing the Journey

There is something surreal about coming to the end of a journey, especially when that journey is long and rough. I can think of many stories told, many movies made, and many accounts in history of difficult and dangerous journeys taken by ordinary people like you and me. Those ordinary people somehow became full of bravery and strength and finished strong. It's no coincidence that the most inspiring stories of those who finished their journey well did so because they were not alone. And when they came to the end, they looked back on that long, treacherous journey and remembered the dangers it brought, the rugged terrains they crossed, and the load they carried.

They recalled the failures, the near death experiences, the little victories, and the motivation that stayed ahead of them that gently called out, "Persevere! Don't give up!" Legends are made of such people. Each of these stories had a motivation for the characters involved—something they were able to fix their eyes upon and keep going. Sometimes one slipped and fell, but the others were always there to pick him up.

The stories that inspire me most are the ones that end with applause. For some reason the roar of applause for a dangerous and difficult job finally completed sends my emotions into orbit. I began writing this book by taking you to Hebrews, and since I love symmetry, I'd like to finish with Hebrews.

Imagine with me coming to the end of your long, treacherous journey of the Christian life. You've slipped from time to time. Perhaps you have even fallen hard, but the other metochoi around you helped you back on your feet so you could keep going along with them toward the prize. With the encouragement of the other metochoi around you and the guiding of the Holy Spirit within you, you submitted well, fought hard, persevered, and followed the Spirit, and now you are at your end.

You wondered many times how to continue, and you were reminded many times that it's by faith. Here, the author of Hebrews brings us to this point. He brings back to life the long list of many ordinary people like you and me, who slipped, fell, got back up, and completed their journey to freedom. He says over and over again that it is by faith that they persevered! Despite the persecution many received, despite the sins they committed, God's mercy and grace supplied the strength and the forgiveness they needed to keep going. The author writes about all this to remind us of who those people of faith were, and then he breaks out in glorious speech driving home this great message straight to our hearts. Let's read from Hebrews 12:

> **¹Therefore we also, since we are surrounded by so great a cloud of witnesses, let us lay aside every weight, and the sin which so easily ensnares us, and let us run with endurance the race that is set before us, ²looking unto Jesus, the author and finisher of our faith, who for the joy that was set before Him endured the cross, despising the shame, and has sat down at the right hand of the throne of God.**

Can you hear them? It's as if they are cheering us onward. The lives they lived are applauding us, shouting out, "Cast off the load of your sin!" "Don't give up!" "You can do it!" They call out with great joy because they know what freedom is—they've journeyed there. Now, I'm not saying this text suggests the previous faithful are watching us, but the lives they lived do call out to us from the Scriptures. The lives they lived during the Old Testament days proclaim God's faithfulness and their faithfulness.

But the motivation—oh, the motivation for us! He was there at the very beginning of our faith. He is the Author of it. He's the One Who will be at the finish line of our journey. He's the Finisher of it, and He finished it perfectly. And He won't be empty-handed. In His hands will be something that motivated Him to persevere through the crucifixion, and He will be waiting to give it to us. It's His joy. His joy was to be at the right hand of His Father in heaven.

Paul wrote in Philippians 2:5-11 that the Father exalted Jesus after Jesus faithfully obeyed the Father. That exaltation was Jesus' joy that was set before Him. Guess what, men— Jesus wants to exalt us. His joy will be given to us in the form of rewards if we become His metochoi—His partakers—His close companions because of our faith. When Jesus was on earth, He spoke of rewards for the faithful more than He spoke of anything else. His joy will be ours forever if we persevere! All those who trusted in Jesus will be with Him forever, and all those Christians who persevered will be rewarded

Verse two says "the joy that *was set* before Him." Do you see that? The joy was already in place, calling Him to endure the cross. And He finished it. He even said, "It is finished!" Jesus has set the course to freedom. He authored it, and He finished it. He knows where to go, where to turn right and where to turn left along the journey.

Stop setting your own course. We don't have to blaze a new trail. He's already made that course. Having already completed it, Jesus is showing us the way to freedom. And He has established His body on earth, the Church—our 70—to walk this journey together. And here's the mindbender: Unless the Lord calls you home before you finish reading this book, you are not at your end. You still have life to live on this earth. The good news is freedom from sin's power can be ours now.

When you trusted Jesus as your Savior, He gave His life to you—you didn't give Him anything. His life is freedom. There are no nails in Jesus. Nothing has Him bound anymore. He already endured that torture. His life is freedom. So when you trusted in Him, He gave you His life, and that life set you free from the penalty of sin. Now, as you submit to Him in obedience, following Him, you are living as you are—free from the power of sin. With His Spirit to convict, comfort, and conform you from the inside, and His Body to connect, care for, and carry you from the outside, you have what it takes to live in the freedom of Christ Jesus. And when you do come to your end, He'll be waiting for you with His joyful rewards for your life of faithfulness on this earth.

You see, men, anyone who trusts in Jesus alone will enter into heaven one day. But not all who trust in Him will become His metochoi. Not all Christians will receive the rewards that Jesus wants to give at the end. His Word says we all will stand before Him at the Judgment (2 Cor. 5:9-10). Why? It's for two reasons: 1) because we trusted in Jesus alone for our salvation—we made it to the Judgment, and 2) because He will judge us according to our faithfulness on earth so He can joyfully reward those who faithfully followed Him.

So the next time you are sitting in the worship service of your church, don't forget those guys on the fringe. Don't forget the others who need to be carried for a while on their life's journey.

Overcomers overcome together—never alone. Pursue authentic fellowship with them, and show them how it leads them on their journey to freedom. Pass it along.

DISCUSSION QUESTIONS

These questions are designed for a small group of men to discuss together after reading each chapter. The purpose is for accountability, openness, authenticity, and purity.

Introduction

1. Why does it usually take getting caught to bring our struggles into the open?
2. What does it really mean to let yourself be known?
3. Do you really believe others share our struggles, or do you think you're the only one?

Chapter One

1. What do you think is/are prerequisite(s) in the life of a man before he can be a metochoi?
2. How do you feel about a Christian man who would turn away from God in his actions?
3. Why do you think many men resist a life together of support and accountability?

Chapter Two

1. If you grew up in a home without supportive parents, how do you learn what grace, acceptance, and fellowship look like?
2. In their churches, do you think most men focus too much on the wrong things, or too little on the right things? Are those the same or different?
3. Have you undervalued fellowship as you've defined it? How can that definition change, if it needs to?
4. Why do we often bring up important/difficult subjects everywhere except church?
5. Are you the kind of person with whom people share their hearts? Why or why not?

Chapter Three

1. What's the best way to become passionate about peoples' needs?
2. How do you go about changing your focus from programs and preferences to people?
3. Have you ever felt like your priorities within the church were missing the mark? What issues are you willing to fight over, and is that a good list or not?

Chapter Four

1. Do you obey God in order to achieve close fellowship, or because you already have it?
2. Have you had relationships where love was conditional on your behavior? How does this relate to your relationship with God?
3. What do you think would happen if you confessed your specific sins and struggles to another man or small group of men?
4. What are the reasons we don't confess to one another? Are these reasons valid?

Chapter Five

1. Is it enough for you to have a plan that only you know about? Is your plan more effective when you tell others about it? Why or why not?
2. Do you have friendships with certain men that look different from those with most other men you know? What makes them different?
3. What are the common components present in all four groups: 70, 12, 3, and 1?
4. Is it harder for you to affirm/encourage other people or to be affirmed/encouraged? Why?
5. You would share certain things with your 3 or 1 that you don't share with your 70 or 12. How do you separate what you share with your 3 or 1 and not with your 70 or 12 without feeling dishonest or lacking in transparency?

Chapter Six

1. If fear is a powerless shadow, why does it paralyze you in certain moments? And how can you respond to it?
2. What is the worst thing that could happen to you by being a champion for accountability?

Chapter Seven

1. How can your accountability be different than that of people who lie and hide their sin? If this has been your style of accountability, how can you change it?
2. How does being truthful protect you?
3. Is the righteousness mentioned in Ephesians 6 simply the deeds you do, or is it something more? If so, what?
4. How does what you believe affect how you act?
5. How can you remove what needs to be removed without reverting to moralism, or righteousness based on works?

Chapter Eight

1. What aspects of Greg's story do you relate to? Do you hear some of your own fears expressed in what he shared?
2. Do you think if your deepest secret was revealed that life could be OK?

Chapter Nine

1. How can living truthfully and with transparency help "the others?"
2. How can you make sure that others who struggle within your church can know of the hope that comes from authentic fellowship?

ENDNOTES

1. Timothy C. Morgan, *Christianity Today,* "Porn's Stranglehold." March, 2008.
2. James D. G. Dunn, *Word Biblical Commentary, Romans 9-16 38B* (Word Books, Dallas, 1988), 874-75.
3. "Agape" is the Greek word translated as "love." It comes only from God (God is love) and is the all-giving, sacrificial love that Christians are commanded to enjoy and spread.
4. Steve Farrar, *Finishing Strong: Going the Distance for Your Family* (Multnomah Publishers, Sisters, Oregon, 1995), 184.
5. Except for church covenant, or doctrinal issues.
6. Drs. Frank B. Minirth and Paul D. Meier, *Happiness Is a Choice* (Baker Book House, Grand Rapids, 1978), 112-113.
7. Granted, they had just witnessed the Transfiguration! Surely they were still coming down from this spiritual high, when the Samaritans were indignant to their Master. I'm sure I would have said the same.
8. International Standard Bible Encyclopedia, Electronic Database Copyright © 1996, 2003, 2006 by Biblesoft, Inc. All rights reserved.

9. Also see Phil. 2:12 where *salvation* is used for a believer to be delivered from the power of sin and not the penalty of sin.
10. Dave and Neta Jackson, *Hero Tales* (Bethany House Publishers, Minneapolis, 1996), 153-154. Also cited on www.nationalgeographic.com/railroad.